**Puzzle Trail**

Who stole the Puzzle...

Who is the Conundrum Castle murderer?

What's been buried on Puzzle Island?

Read on to find the answers to these and many other tantalising puzzles. But first you have to outwit master puzzler Clive Doig by solving the clues on each page. And things aren't always that straightforward...

# Puzzle Trail

---

**Clive Doig**
*Illustrated by Malcolm Bird*

**BBC/KNIGHT BOOKS**

Copyright © British Broadcasting Corporation 1984
Illustrations copyright © British Broadcasting Corporation 1984

*First published 1984 by*
*BBC/Knight Books*

**British Library C.I.P.**

Doig, Clive
  Puzzle trail.
  1. Puzzles – Juvenile literature
  I. Title
  793.73      GV1493

ISBN 0-340-36193-X
     0-563-20336-6 (BBC)

---

*The characters and situations in this book are entirely imaginary and bear no relation to any real person or actual happening*

This book is sold subject to the condition that it shall not, by way of trade or otherwise, be lent, re-sold, hired out or otherwise circulated without the publisher's prior consent in any form of binding or cover other than that in which it is published and without a similar condition including this condition being imposed on the subsequent purchaser.

Printed and bound in Great Britain for the British Broadcasting Corporation, 35 Marylebone High Street, London W1M 4AA and Hodder and Stoughton Paperbacks, a division of Hodder and Stoughton Ltd, Mill Road, Dunton Green, Sevenoaks, Kent (Editorial Office: 47 Bedford Square, London, WC1 3DP) by Cox and Wyman Ltd, Reading. Photoset by Rowland Phototypesetting Ltd, Bury St Edmunds, Suffolk.

# CONTENTS

| | |
|---|---|
| Introduction | 6 |
| PUZZLE ISLAND | 9 |
| What animal did I meet? | 20 |
| Who are wearing the scarves? | 21 |
| LOST AND FOUND | 23 |
| Girl's Bingo | 54 |
| Who committed the murder? | 55 |
| Cheat! | 56 |
| THE PUZZLETON PLANS | 59 |
| Odd ones out | 90 |
| Decode it! | 91 |
| THE RIDDLE OF SKULLY ISLAND | 93 |
| Picture pairs | 101 |
| Round up | 102 |
| ANSWERS | 104 |

# INTRODUCTION

*Puzzle Trail* first appeared on BBC 1 in the autumn of 1980. The five programmes in that series were broadcast from Monday to Friday each day, and with Andy Johnson and Donna Reeve leading the way. Clues and adventures led to the whereabouts of a secret and unusual treasure. The response from the viewers was enormous; more than 12,000 correct solutions poured in during the week. The sender of the first correct postcard received the actual treasure.

Each year since then BBC 1 has continued to show a succession of *Puzzle Trails* of different kinds. The aim has remained the same – for viewers to deduce from clues in the sketches and poems where a hidden treasure, message or object is.

In 1981 Tommy Boyd and Sally Grace went on the Puzzle Trail in the search for something that Tommy had lost. He knew all thirty-six places he had been to and retraced his steps place by place until he found where it was. Many viewers beat Tommy to it and discovered the answer before the last of the five programmes.

In 1983 Kirsty Miller and Howard Stableford presented *The Puzzleton Plans*, a mystery which took three weeks to solve and involved twelve suspects to a burglary in the town of Puzzleton. Highly secret plans were stolen and one of the inhabitants of the town had done it. Kirsty and Howard played all the suspects as well as themselves.

Puzzle Trail returned with a Treasure Hunt and *The Riddle of Skully Island*. Davy Jones (of The Monkees fame) and Eileen Fletcher try and find the hidden treasure and keep meeting strange characters, who look remarkably like themselves.

Like the TV programmes, which day by day give clues to where the treasure is, the Puzzle Trails in this book give the clues page by page. By the end of each chapter you will have enough information to be able to solve the puzzle.

If you can remember all the solutions to the Puzzle Trails from the TV it may be a little easier for you, but I have changed some of the clues and answers around.

*The Riddle of Skully Island* is to be shown on the screen in 1984. The written version is practically identical but there are some differences, so working it out in the book, or looking up the answers at the back, will not give you the answer for the TV puzzle or vice-versa.

I've also included some other one-page puzzles for you to work out. Some of them are dead easy, the others are excruciatingly difficult.

*Clive Doig*
Devisor and writer PUZZLE TRAIL

# PUZZLE TRAIL

Each Puzzle Trail begins with a map, grid or plan.

This you should always use in conjunction with the clues, crossing out as you wish.

All clues that are given in the text are numbered in the left-hand margin, so that you will not miss anything. These numbers are helpful when you are working out the solutions from the answers.

Good Luck! And on with the trails . . .

# **PUZZLE ISLAND**

\* \* \* \*

## FIND WHERE THE TREASURE IS AND WHAT IT IS

# KEY TO SYMBOLS USED ON MAP:

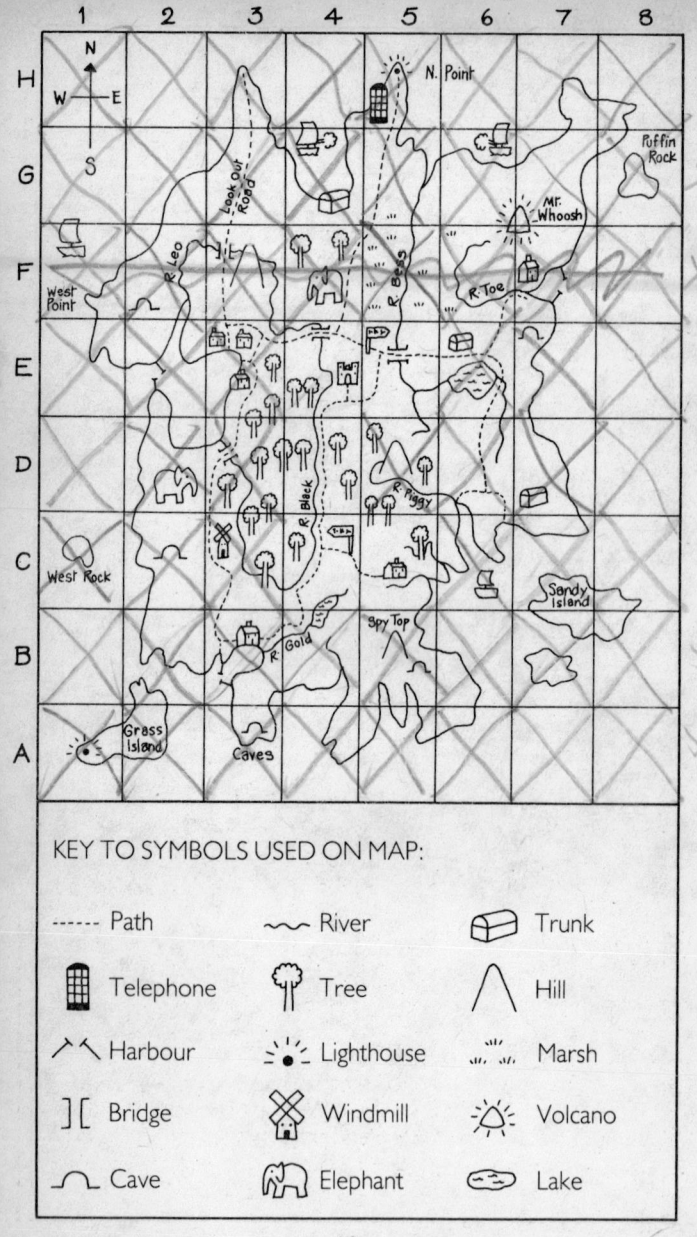

- ------ Path
- ~~~ River
- 🗄 Trunk
- 📞 Telephone
- 🌳 Tree
- ⋀ Hill
- ⋏⋏ Harbour
- ☀ Lighthouse
- ،،، Marsh
- ][ Bridge
- ⋈ Windmill
- ☼ Volcano
- ⌒ Cave
- 🐘 Elephant
- ⌬ Lake

10

# PUZZLE ISLAND

Andy and Donna went to the mysterious Puzzle Island to try and find the treasure. Can you follow the clues and discover where on the island it is hidden?

They landed at Great Harbour, where they met a funny old pirate called Short John Gold. Short John Gold gave them a number of clues to where on Puzzle Island the special treasure was hidden. See if you can work out where the treasure is hidden as well, and also what the treasure is.

This is Short John Gold's first clue.
   PIRATE: Well, my hearties, you want to know where the treasure is, eh? I tell thee it's hidden *somewhere on dry land* shown on the map.

You can use the map to cross out the squares where the treasure *isn't*, for instance you could start by crossing out squares H1, H2, H6, G1, F8 and others where there is no dry land in the squares (see clue 1). Use the map again to follow Short John Gold's clues.

PIRATE: Ho-ho, my hearties, I expect you be wondering
2 what the treasure is? Well, I can tell thee it is *hard and*
3 *shiny* and it has got *four legs*. But be warned! Somewhere on the map there is an island which is known as 'Little Rock'. Not many people know that. Now, there are killer sharks swimming all round that island, and it is very dangerous in those squares. I can tell you for free the
4 treasure is *not in any of the squares that surround Little Rock square*. It's far too dangerous!

What is more, shipmates, horror upon horrors, in the north of the island there is a man-eating lion at large. It
5 lives in the northernmost cave and roams freely in *all the squares that lie next to its home square whether they be diagonally or up or down or across from it*. Those squares are not safe, no treasure there!

Methinks we better go south down that path to the windmill.

As the pirate journeyed to the windmill to get out of the lion's clutches he offered more clues to the location of the treasure.

6 PIRATE: *The treasure is in a trunk*, my dears, in a trunk,
7 and *it is in a square with water in it*, of course, that could be the sea, a river or a lake.

The treasure is not very big, you know, it can fit into a
8 box that is only *22cm × 15cm × 15cm*. Funnily enough it
9 is *worth more to you broken than unbroken*.

If you look closely at the Puzzle Island map you will find that some of the rivers and paths have names. It might be helpful to you to know where the pirate meant when he said:

PIRATE: The other day, I was at Look-out point, looking out over the sea, when this mermaid swims up and says to me that she has been in the same square as where the treasure is hidden, that very day. That's a long way to
10 swim, thought I, but she ups and says that *she didn't swim through more than thirteen squares, including the treasure square and the Look-out square, to get from there to me.* Swimming all the way.

11 You know, just like the mermaid, *the treasure is brightly*
12 *coloured* and like her *it has an interesting tale, or should I say tail attached to it.*

PIRATE: You'll never guess what, my hearties! The old volcano, that's Mount Whoosh, has just erupted fearfully
13 and covered *all the land in the top nine north-east squares of the map* with molten lava. You will be glad to know the treasure is not in any of those squares.

PIRATE: Let us now go further south from Big Harbour on E3 and visit another harbour.

With which he followed the path past the windmill down to the harbour, one of the three harbours on the island.

13

**PIRATE:** Well, shiver me timbers! Not a moment too
14 soon! The windmill has just caught fire, *destroyed that square and spread north two squares* and destroyed those too. Lucky we got to the safety of this harbour. The elephant on square D2 was quite lucky too, nearly got his trunk singed.

By the way, when you find the treasure, you will find
15 it is *itself quite a collector's item*.

If you have followed all the clues to where the treasure isn't you should by this point in the search have crossed off about 40 of the 64 squares on the map.

The more up-to-date map opposite that Short John Gold found at the harbour is very helpful because it has all the squares where the treasure cannot be found crossed off.

The pirate complimented Andy and Donna on getting very close and doing so well, but they hadn't finished the search, and nor have you. Short John Gold had a lot more clues up his sleeve.

**PIRATE:** Listen to this my beauties, the square where the
16 treasure is hidden is *the same distance from Spyglass Hill as it is from Little Harbour*. I hope you understand that.

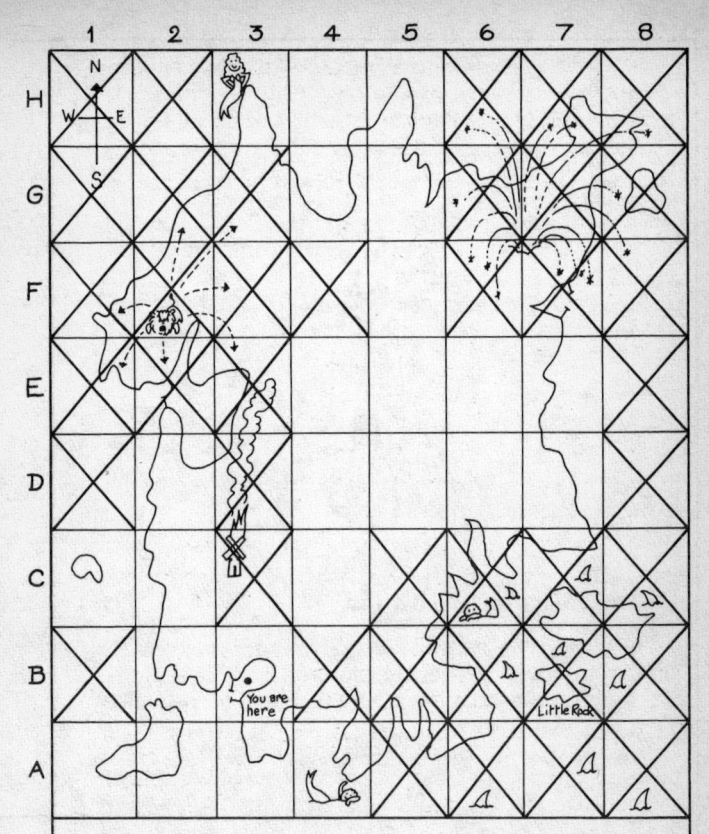

Of course, Short John Gold didn't say which hill was Spyglass Hill (not Spytop Hill) or which harbour was Little Harbour. You can check the symbols for hill and harbour in the map key on page 10.

Short John Gold then said it would be better if everyone went to the Black Knight's Castle, especially as the evil lord was on holiday. It was not a moment too soon.

17  PIRATE: What a bit of luck, shipmates, *the square directly to the north of the square with a lone tree in it* has been totally overrun by huge ants, so that square is eliminated. Oh yes, there is another square you can eliminate
18  straight away my dears, that is *the square with all the marsh in it*, it also has quicksand there and is totally impassable.

15

If you have not guessed what the treasure is yet, here is another of old Short John Gold's clues:

19  PIRATE: The treasure sometimes *squeaks or rattles* and it
20  can be found *in a farmyard or on a mantelpiece*.

By the way, I shouldn't look to the east if I were you. There is a horrible monster lurking in the lake we call
21  Lake Bess. It is called the Loch Bess Monster, so the *lake square and the next square downstream* must be crossed out unless you want to be gobbled up.

PIRATE: While we are here at the castle you might like
22  to know that the treasure square is just *two knight's moves away from the castle square*.

In chess the pieces called knights move in a special way across the chess board. The knight moves by jumping to a square that is two across and one down or two up and one across from the starting point. For example the knight on E4 in the diagram below can only go to squares G3, G5, F2, F6, D2, D6, C3 or C5 on its first move.

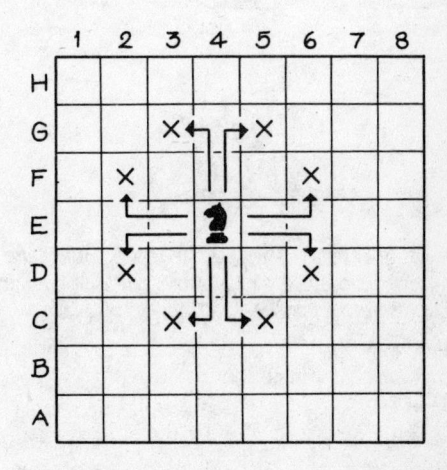

What else did the silly old pirate have to say?

23  PIRATE: The treasure is a little bit like a little toe. *A little toe that is by a river.*

If you have correctly deduced all the pirate's clever clues including that last one, you should know roughly what the treasure is and be down to about seven squares where it could possibly be.

Short John Gold still had a few more clues to the right square however:

PIRATE: Blow my braces to the wind, it's the lighthouse, the offshore lighthouse, it's gone out! Well, you landlubbers might not understand, but that spells doom
24 to us pirates and smugglers and the like, no ship is safe. *All squares in the same column or row as that lighthouse* must be eliminated from your reckoning. Oh! Did I ever tell
25 you that *no path or road enters the square* where the treasure is?

Another disaster is that a hurricane, Hurricane Nellie, has swept across the south of the island. It has devastated
26 *all squares with a coastline that faces south.*

Terrible things seem to happen on Puzzle Island, perhaps the only safe place is where the treasure is.

PIRATE: That's right, shipmates, more bad news, two
27 pirate ships are fighting each other in the north. *All squares with land between the two ships* have been heavily bombarded and must be excluded.

I'll give you a grand clue now, my hearties, I used to
28 stand *midway between the bridge and the sails facing the sunset*, and in that position the treasure was directly behind me.

There are, of course, four bridges on the map and five squares with sails in them.

Over to Short John Gold for the last of his clues:

> PIRATE: The last clue, shipmates. You know that you can get to the treasure square by sea and river, but I'm here to tell you that that very square which is the answer to
29 the whole puzzle *does not have a coastline in it.*
>
> Now you know where the treasure is, you see, I told you it was in a trunk, do you know what
30 the treasure is? It possibly *needs some 'oinkment'*
31 and it is also *a greedy miser* because
32 *it is easy to put things in it but difficult to take them out.*

If after all those clues you still do not know what the treasure is or what square it has been hidden in, you can turn to the answers on page 104 where all will be explained.

# WHAT ANIMAL DID I MEET?

As I was walking down the street I suddenly came face to face with one of the animals you can see above. But I didn't know what sort of animal it was, I could not remember its name. Of course I did know it was either a lion or a leopard or a camel or an elephant or a giraffe or an ape or a squirrel.
'Give me a clue, what's your name?' I asked.
'Guess,' the beast replied.
'Noel?' I guessed.
'No!' it growled.
'Are you an ape?' quizzed I, staring intently at the animal.
'Well, I have got two-thirds of an ape inside me,' it replied.
'Oh you cruel thing, how greedy!' I shouted.
'No, no, no, no. That's a clue, it's not the animal inside me.'
'Oh, I see, of course not; now I know who you are!' I said.
Do you know the animal I was talking to?

# WHO ARE WEARING THE SCARVES?

Six ladies waiting at a bus stop. Can you find out the names of the two who are wearing scarves from the information below?
Annie is at one end.
Betty is wearing a skirt.
Carla has boots on.
Deirdre is not wearing a hat.
Emma is not wearing a coat.
Freda has not got a handbag.
Carla is not smiling.
Emma has not got a shopping bag.

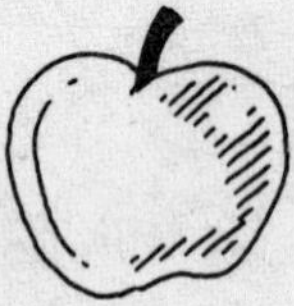

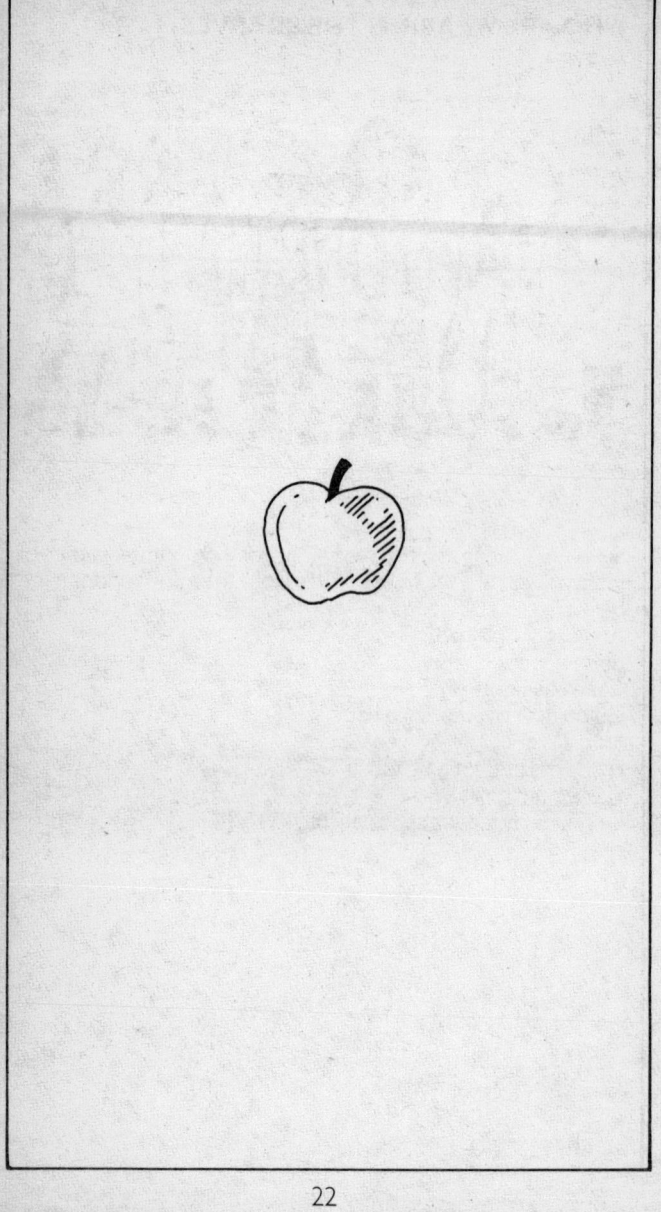

# **LOST AND FOUND**

* * * *

WORK OUT WHAT VALUABLE
OBJECT HAS BEEN LOST
AND WHERE IT IS

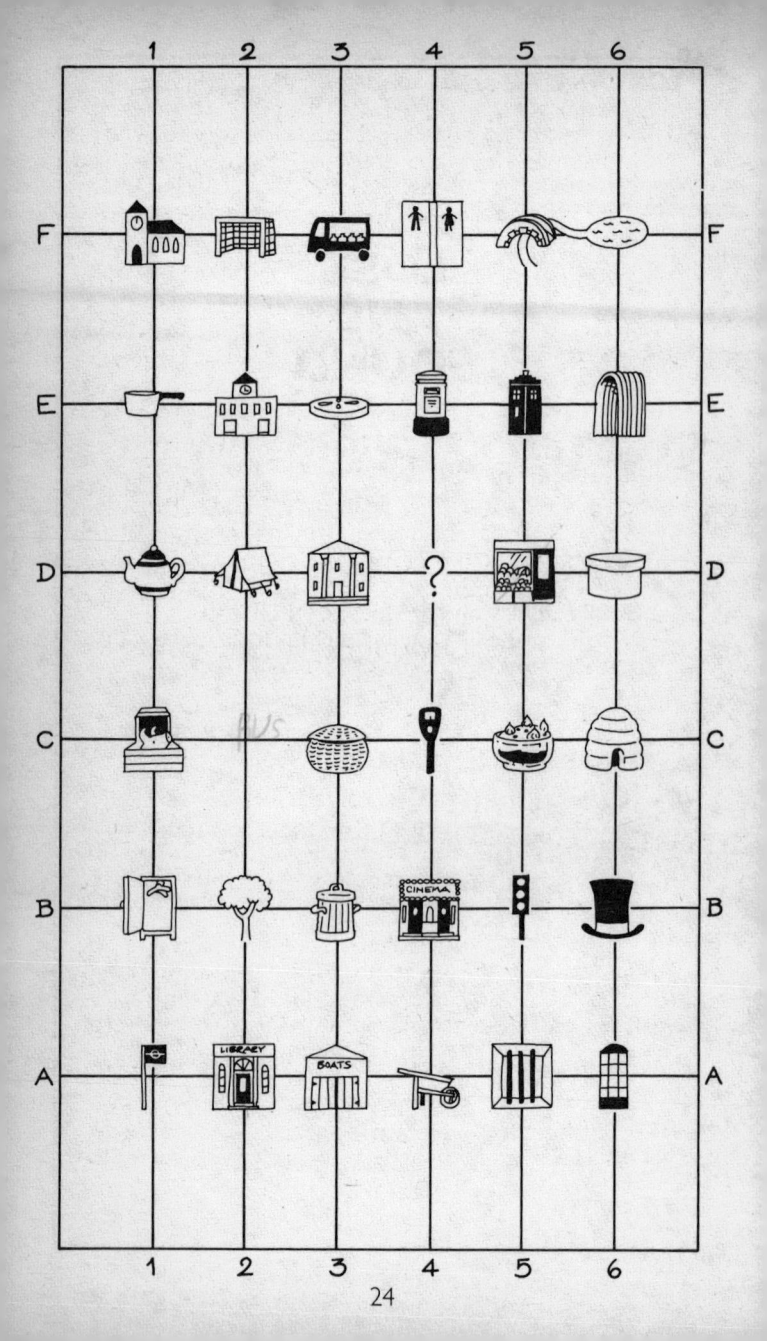

24

# LOST AND FOUND

Tommy started another Puzzle Trail by saying that he had lost something very precious. You have to try to find out what it is he has lost and where he could have lost it. This Puzzle Trail is full of tricks, puzzles, brain-teasers and clues. There will be clues, conundrums and some very useless information to help and hinder you on your way.

When you mislay something the best way to find it is to retrace your steps to all the places you have been, and see if it is at any of them. This is exactly what Tommy did, and he had to remember exactly where he had been and in what order. To help him, and you, here is a list of all the places and things he had recently been to. Some of them are quite ordinary and others a little strange:

Church, Goalposts, Milk-float, Toilets, Bridge, Pond, School, Saucepan, Manhole, Letter Box, Prison, Telephone Box, Police Box, Workman's Hut, Teapot, Tent, Town Hall, Greengrocers, Hatbox, Pigsty, Bus, Sewing Basket, Parking Meter, Trifle, Beehive, Wardrobe, Tree, Dustbin, Cinema, Traffic Lights, Top Hat, Bus Stop, Library, Boathouse, Wheelbarrow.

All the places and things where Tommy could have mislaid his precious object, he positioned on the intersections of a grid. Your grid is on page 24.

*1* The grid makes it easier to trace his way back from the starting point, marked '?' at intersection D4, down all the lines or roads marked A, B, C, D, E, F, 1, 2, 3, 4, 5 and 6. There is one thing missing from the grid at C2, can you find out what it is from the list above?

The first thing that Tommy did, of course, was to look for his missing thing at home(D4 the ?). He looked in an old trunk, because that is where the last Puzzle Trail treasure had been found, but all that was in there were:

*2* *roller skates, radio, ruler, rubber, rugby ball, rattle, ribbons, rabbit* and *calendar.*

But not the thing he was looking for. Can you notice that one of the things in the trunk is different from all the others? More about that later.

Tommy had definitely lost whatever it was, it was nowhere in his home, so he had to start retracing his steps and so have you. He started to munch an apple to help him think.

Now, where had he bought the apple?

If you look at the grid of all the places, you will be able to see where he had just come from. Along one of the lines from D4 is the place he must have bought the apple. So he went back there.

# THE GREENGROCER'S SHOP

That's right, the greengrocer's shop. Had he lost his ?? there? He spoke to the shopkeeper.

TOMMY: Hello again, I've lost something and I wondered if you'd found it anywhere?

SHOPKEEPER: Oh no. I've been to lunch since you were here and emptied all my boxes, it's not in amongst the fruit. Wait a minute though, I did find this little shiny button on the floor.

3 TOMMY: No, *it isn't as small as that*. Thank you all the same.

SHOPKEEPER: I've found nothing bigger, sorry.

TOMMY: Oh well, can't be here then. Can I buy another apple?

SHOPKEEPER: You wouldn't like to buy any:

4 *peaches* or *pomegranates* or *oranges* or *potatoes* or *plums* or *parsnips* or even *pears* would you?

TOMMY: That's odd, in fact one of those is very odd. No, thank you, I'll just have another apple, please.

SHOPKEEPER: Certainly, remember, an apple a day keeps the doctor away.

TOMMY: Doctor who?

SHOPKEEPER: Exactly.

TOMMY: That's a clue, Doctor Who!

And it was a clue that the shopkeeper had given. A clue to the last place that Tommy had come from. *Doctor Who?*

If you look back at the grid again you will see why. The greengrocer's shop is at D5 and going directly up line 5 there is . . .

4    5    6

F

E

D

# THE POLICE BOX

The *Tardis*!

Well, actually it is an old police box. Dr Who's time machine has always been a police box since he first appeared on BBC TV over twenty years ago. Sadly, you do not see the old police boxes on the roadside any more – the 'bobby' on his beat used to use them to call his local station, but now, of course, policemen have two-way radios.

Mind you, if the public wanted to call a policeman, all they had to do was pick up the phone behind the panel and one would come immediately. Suddenly a policeman, PC55, appeared in front of Tommy.

    PC55: Can I help you, young man?

    TOMMY: Yes, I've lost something, and I wondered if anything had been handed in at the station?

    PC55: Let's see, what has been handed in today:
5 *camera, car, coat, mackintosh, coins, cross, clock.*

    TOMMY: No, the thing I've lost is none of those, though
6 *all those things seem very similar except one.*

    PC55: Could be a clue, couldn't it? Anyway, I must get back to work. Bye bye!

To Tommy's surprise there was a weird noise and the police box just disappeared into thin air. Maybe it had been the Tardis! Anyway, he knew and you now know, that whatever he had lost was not in there, nor was it at the shop.

If you look back again at the grid on page 24 you will see that the Tardis, *sorry!* the police box, was at E5. Tommy had three ways to go to retrace his steps, either to the letter box on E4, the bridge at F5 or the workman's hut at E6.

Suddenly he remembered, he'd had a cup of tea with someone just before he had been to the police box. No, he couldn't have got any tea at the bridge over the river, nor from a pillar box, so it must have been . . .

29

# THE WORKMAN'S HUT

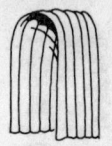

Yes, Tommy had had a long chat and a cup of char with the workman inside his roadside hut. He went back there and asked the workman whether he'd left anything behind:

> WORKMAN: 'Oh, no. I remember distinct like, sir. You came here dripping wet, because you had fallen into some water. Well, you emptied your pockets and dried
> 7 off in front of my brazier. I remember you had a *bunch of keys, a dirty handkerchief, an old pencil, a rubber* and *thirty-five pence* in change. I put it in a tin and you took the lot away when you were dry.

> TOMMY: So I must have lost it before I came and had a cup of tea with you.

> WORKMAN: 'Seems likely, that does. Would you like another cuppa?

> TOMMY: No, thank you, I had better get on with my search. By the way, Mr Workman, what are you working on?

> WORKMAN: I works on all sorts of things, you know, it's roads here, but I also work on:
> 8 *pavements, railways, river beds, rubbish tips, roundabouts, ring roads, runways.*

> TOMMY: I see, quite an 'RRRR'd worker you R.

> WORKMAN: Very droll, very droll. But I'll tell you one thing, young sir. I bet the place you lost your
> 9 thingywhat's-it *has a T* in it. Always got to have a T.

With which the workman went back to his tea, and Tommy went on his way.

There was a fine clue in what the workman said to where Tommy had been just before the workman's hut. Something to do with being soaking wet. Tommy had obviously just got very wet. Probably fallen in somewhere . . . where?

# THE POND

Poor old Tommy had tripped over a fishing line and gone headlong ... *splash!* ... into the pond on F6. He could have easily lost his thingammyjig in the water. When he got back there to investigate he found what the fisherman had pulled up from the pond:

10 *boots, brick, bedspring, bell, anchor, basin, bicycle.*

No fish, just all that rubbish. At least one of those things was rather different from all the others. Yet another clue!

Tommy started throwing the things back into the pond, when out of the shimmering water rose a very beautiful but angry Water Nymph. She was very cross with Tommy.

WATER NYMPH: What are you doing? I've just been clearing out the bottom of my pond. All that rubbish messing up my nice pool. I fixed it all to the end of the fisherman's line, now you come along and chuck it all back.

TOMMY: Sorry, Miss Water Nymph. While you have been clearing out down there, I wonder whether you've found anything belonging to me?

WATER NYMPH: I don't know, what does it look like?

11 TOMMY: Well, *it's something bright and shiny.*

WATER NYMPH: The only thing that is bright and shiny down here are the little fishies and me.

So Tommy's bright and shiny thingy could not have been lost in the pond. He thanked the water nymph and helped lift out all the rubbish again and went on his way.

Well, as you can see, the only way that Tommy could go was straight along the F road to the bridge at F5.

# THE BRIDGE

Tommy could have dropped it over the bridge into the river, but he decided he had not, because he would have heard the splash. But if he had dropped it *it would have floated off in the opposite direction to the one it was pointing.*

While he was standing there contemplating, a little old lady came up to him.

OLD LADY: Hullo, Tommy, I believe you have lost something?

TOMMY: That's right, can you help?

OLD LADY: Of course I can dear, I can give you a clue to where it is with one of my little poems, would you like to hear it?

TOMMY: Yes please.

OLD LADY: *Since you're here, I'll tell you this,*
*'Ere you came, I saw your quest.*
*Within my mind, the place appeared,*
*It is not far, it is not near,*
*Near or far, you'll soon find out,*
*Grandma knows, without a doubt.*

With which she went on her way. That was not the only time the little old lady will appear in this Puzzle Trail. More poem clues from her later.

Her poem actually tells you that the place that you and Tommy are looking for is neither near the bridge nor far from it.

***********************************************************
## DID YOU KNOW...
that the oldest bridge in the world is in Turkey and is over 2800 years old?

One of the newest is the Humber Bridge in England. Its main towers are so tall that they are 35mm further apart at the top than they are at the bottom. This is because of the curvature of the earth!

***********************************************************


Enough about bridges, Tommy's whatyermacallit was certainly not at the bridge on F5.

And so far we know he did not leave it at the shop, the police box, the workman's hut or the pond. There are two clues to
WHERE IT IS
*It has a T in it (9).*
*It is neither near or far from the bridge (14).*
There are also two clues to
WHAT IT IS
*It is larger than a button (3).*
*It is bright and shiny (11)*

Now, what is the only place that Tommy could have come from to reach the bridge?

# THE TOILETS

Have you ever noticed how difficult it often is to tell who's who on the little signs on the doors? Men or women, girls or boys, lords or ladies, water nymphs or daleks!

Toilets has a T in it so they could be the place, but Tommy remembered he had been so confused by the signs that he had not gone in to the public toilets, so he could not have lost anything there.

************************************************************

## DID YOU KNOW...

that the first flushing public toilets were built in Fleet Street in 1852. They were called 'Public Waiting Rooms', and advertisements were put in *The Times* and 50,000 leaflets were handed out to explain their use.

But after two months only fifty-eight people had used them. As they cost two pence to use, it was probably considered too much to pay for spending a penny. It wasn't until 1893 that it cost only one P. to have another.

************************************************************

Where had Tommy come from to get to the toilets? The milk float has a T in it. But it was another kind of letter that had been important at the last place he had been to. A letter that Mr Bathurst, Tommy's old schoolteacher had asked him to post. Of course, at E4 is

34

# THE LETTER BOX

You could also call it a post-box or a pillar box.

When Tommy was posting Mr Bathurst's letter he could
15 have accidentally dropped the thing he lost *through the slot* in the top with the letter. Luckily for Tommy as he was standing by the letter box along came a postman to empty it for collection. Tommy naturally asked him if there was anything else in the post-box other than letters.

POSTMAN: It's amazing what gets dropped into letter boxes. As well as all the letters just look at this lot:
16 *wristwatch, wallet, wire, washers, wood, wet wiggly worms, whatyermacallits* and even *sausages*.
It's disgraceful!

TOMMY: Seems to be an odd letter in there somewhere.

17 POSTMAN: Oh, which one's that, then? This one addressed to somebody *in Canada*?

TOMMY: No, that's the letter I was posting for Mr Bathurst. I say, did you say whatyermacallits, you've found a whatyermacallit in there?

POSTMAN: Not a whatyermacallit, it's a woggle!

TOMMY: A woggle? Oh, I know, the girl guide I met at the tent earlier must have dropped that in there. So my whatsit isn't there, oh dear!

POSTMAN: Sorry young man. I must be off now.

And he went off taking all the letters in his bag to the sorting office.

\*\*\*\*\*\*\*\*\*\*\*\*\*\*\*\*\*\*\*\*\*\*\*\*\*\*\*\*\*\*\*\*\*\*\*\*\*\*\*\*\*\*\*\*\*\*\*\*\*\*\*\*\*\*\*\*\*\*\*\*

## DID YOU KNOW...

that post-boxes were the idea of novelist Anthony Trollope in 1852. The first pillar box was installed in Butchergate, Carlisle in September 1853. Early English pillar boxes were green; red was not introduced until 1874. Many old pillar boxes are protected under law, and are officially 'Listed Buildings'.

\*\*\*\*\*\*\*\*\*\*\*\*\*\*\*\*\*\*\*\*\*\*\*\*\*\*\*\*\*\*\*\*\*\*\*\*\*\*\*\*\*\*\*\*\*\*\*\*\*\*\*\*\*\*\*\*\*\*\*\*

# THE MANHOLE AND ITS COVER

Yes, of course, the manhole is the only place that Tommy could have come from.

The manhole cover was not on the manhole. That could be very dangerous, thought Tommy. A man wearing a protective hat appeared from the hole; he was down there mending the drains.

MAN: Oi! Was it you who dropped summat down my hole?

TOMMY: 'Er, well, it might have been, what was it?

MAN: 'Ere you are, an 'andbag. Just be careful where you drop things in future.

TOMMY: No, no, I didn't drop a handbag.

But the man had disappeared down the hole again. Tommy felt a little tap on his shoulder. It was the little old lady again.

OLD LADY: Oh, there's my handbag, how kind of you to find it, young man. I knew I'd lost it somewhere. Have you found what you are looking for?

TOMMY: No, not yet.

OLD LADY: What is it?

TOMMY: Well, seeing as you ask, I can tell you it's *not my key or my penknife*, and it's *not a buckle or a coin*. But *it is something round*.

OLD LADY: Like the manhole. That's round. Have you discovered where you lost it yet?

TOMMY: Not quite, but I think I'm working towards it. Anyway I thought you knew.

OLD LADY: Oh yes, so I do. I'll give you a few more clues a little later and help you on your way.

With which she daintily skirted round the round manhole and went off in the direction of the town hall.

*********************************************************

### DID YOU KNOW...

that most manholes are round because that is the safest shape they can be, to stop the covers falling down the hole. The diagram below shows that a round lid can't fall through; but with a square hole, the lid could fall through at one angle.

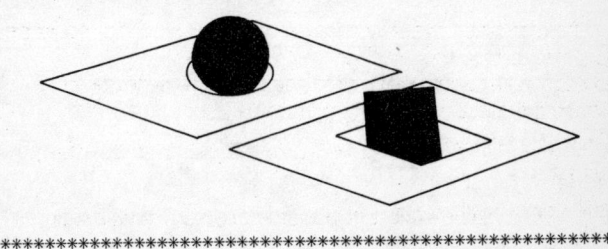

*********************************************************

Have you guessed what the object is that Tommy lost?
Here are the clues so far to
WHAT IT IS
It is larger than a button (3).
It is bright and shiny (11).
It floated off pointing in a different direction (12).
It could go through a letter box (15).
It is round (19).

But it is not a wrist watch, a wallet, a sausage or a woggle (16).
It is not a coin, a buckle, a penknife, or a key (18).

The woggle, which is a ring that a cub scout threads his neckerchief through, belonged to Gertie the Guide.

Now what was Tommy doing just before he crossed the manhole last time he came that way? He had been delivering a letter to the letter box for someone. Someone who is very important in helping you find out the lost object.

20  Mr Bathurst was Tommy's old geography teacher, and his name, *Bathurst*, has great significance when considering the missing object. Geographically speaking, that is!

Where was Mr Bathurst?

# THE SCHOOL

Tommy, of course, had taken the letter to the letter box from the school on E2. He went back there and asked Mr Bathurst whether he had seen him drop anything.

MR BATHURST: Did you post my letter?

TOMMY: Oh, yes sir, but did I drop anything last time I was here?

MR BATHURST: All I remember, young Tom, was that you came here to have a look at my atlas. Something about my name you said.

TOMMY: That's right, Mr Bathurst, a girl guide told me *something very interesting about your name (20)*. I looked it up, and she was correct. I had better go and see her.

MR BATHURST: Never very good at geography, were you? Now, which direction was that?

TOMMY: It was due north, I know.

MR BATHURST: What did I tell you, you're wrong! The girl guide's tent is due south from here.

21 TOMMY: Oh, I know that, I meant *you are due north*.

# THE TENT

Tommy left Mr Bathurst due north of the tent. When he got to D2 Gertie the girl guide popped out of the flap.

GERTIE: Hello, Tommy, sorry I'm in a bit of a flap, I've lost my woggle.

TOMMY: Here it is, Gertie, you dropped it in the letter box. You haven't seen the thing that I lost, have you?

GERTIE: You asked me that last time you were here.

TOMMY: Did I?

GERTIE: Which can only prove you lost it before you came here. *Do you want to borrow mine?*

TOMMY: No thanks, as I'm already travelling south, I know the way. Bye-bye.

Tommy set off south down line 2 to C2. But whatever should have been at C2 was not there; it was off on one of its routes. So Tommy continued south to somewhere else with roots.

# THE TREE

Tommy remembered that when he had been at the tree before, vandals had carved their initials on the bark. He had gone to tell Gertie about it. Trees could be killed by that sort of irresponsible behaviour.

From behind the tree appeared the little old lady. She seemed to be popping up all over the place! She explained that she had visited Tommy's granny at C3 and she had another poem.

23  OLD LADY:

> *Branching out east is your next direction,*
> *Away from this tree at a near intersection,*
> *Seek with your nose the following clue,*
> *Keeping a course that is just straight and true,*
> 24  *Examine the rabbit, his lair and his lunch,*
> 25  *To find out the reason for grandmama's hunch.*

And she disappeared again.

There were a number of clues in her poem, some very important and some possibly a little misleading. Rabbits? Lair? Lunch? Grandmama?

The first thing you can do is find out where Tommy had to go next. . . . *east is your next direction . . . seek with your nose . . .*
Something that is east of the tree on B2 and smelly!

# THE DUSTBIN

Tommy went east to B3 and the dustbin. He emptied the contents, they were certainly smelly.

26 *potato peelings, popcorn packets, pieces of pie, papers, paint, peapods, stubs.*

Yet again there seems to be something odd about one of those things in the dustbin. It was the popcorn packet and the stubs that gave Tommy the clue to where he had been before the dustbin. The stubs were not cigarette stubs, they were cinema ticket stubs that he had thrown away in the bin. . . . *keeping a course . . . straight and true . . .*

# THE CINEMA

One of the films showing at the cinema was a Bugs Bunny. A rabbit! Another film was about the Arctic and was called *The Way to Bathurst* (20). He decided to ask the usherette if she had found anything between the seats.

27 TOMMY: I was sitting in the *third row, third seat in.*

USHERETTE: I always search between the seats with my torch after every performance. No. I just found the usual ice cream cartons, popcorn packets and old shoes. What have you lost?

TOMMY: It's bright and shiny, round, bigger than
28 a button but *not as big as a dustbin lid* and it is
29 *very attractive.*

USHERETTE: Very attractive, eh? No, the only attractive thing I've seen round here is that explorer chap in *'The Way to Bathurst' about the north pole* (20).

TOMMY: By the way, what has a Bugs Bunny film got to do with the place I am looking for?

USHERETTE: *There's a rabbit in it* (24).

# THE WHEELBARROW

Tommy had been at the wheelbarrow before B4.

*************************************************************

## DID YOU KNOW...

that the wheelbarrow was invented in China two thousand years ago. It was called a wooden ox or gliding horse; and it is still used in China today to carry people about. Some wheelbarrows were even fitted with sails, like a junk, to speed them on their way.

*************************************************************

All he found in the wheelbarrow was a note:

30 *Look out for all those 1's and 2's, 3's, 4's and 5's.*

Where are a lot of numbers? The telephone of course, round the dial!

Tommy avoided the prison, because he'd never been inside, and so he came to

# THE TELEPHONE BOX

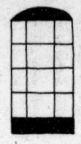

Tommy had been there earlier phoning up his gran. But he had not left anything in there. While he was looking, an escaped prisoner ran by.

PC55 soon arrived, apprehended the prisoner and took him off to prison, Tommy followed.

# THE PRISON

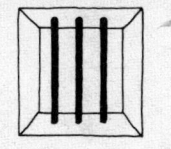

Tommy went to visit the prisoner once he was safely locked up inside. Maybe he had stolen the what's-it?

    TOMMY: Are you inside for stealing?

    PRISONER: Oh no, mate, I'm in here for a sort of musical crime.

    TOMMY: What's that?

    PRISONER: Robbery with violins!

    TOMMY: Very funny. Was it in the news?

31    PRISONER: No, mate. But the *news* has something to do with what you've lost, don't it?

    TOMMY: Yes, I suppose it does. Can you help me find it?

    PRISONER: I could give you some criminal advice as to where to go.
Go and pinch some amber, it's valuable stuff.
Stop will say the cop, that's quite enough.

    TOMMY: Go, amber, stop! Of course . . .

# THE TRAFFIC LIGHTS

Green for go, amber for caution, red for stop.

*********************************************************
## DID YOU KNOW...

that the first type of traffic lights had only two colours. Red for stop and green for caution. They were installed in 1868 opposite the Houses of Parliament, and were gas operated. Unfortunately those first traffic lights blew up injuring the policeman operating them.

*********************************************************

Last time Tommy was at the traffic lights he helped a little old lady across the road. Funnily enough she was there again with another poem:

32 OLD LADY: *Clever Tom, you don't understand*
*The obvious clues I have to hand;*
*Hints to the East I have said,*
*Remember the thing you put on your head.*
*Exit north, the container to see,*
*End up then, with a double B.*

Of course clever Tom did understand, and so should you.

East of the traffic lights is the top hat at B6. If you go north from there you eventually come to the hat box through the beehive. There is another clever clue hidden in the little old lady's poem.

# THE TOP HAT

***********************************************************

### DID YOU KNOW...

that the first time a top hat was worn in public was in 1797 by a Mr Dandy James Hetherington. He was fined fifty pounds, a lot of money in those days, for 'Appearing on the public highway wearing upon his head a tall structure having a shiny lustre and calculated to frighten timid people'.

***********************************************************

But the top hat on B6 is a magic top hat and Tommy found a number of things in it, scarves, flags, sausages, a bouquet of flowers and a rabbit, but not the thing he had lost. Finally, with a great flourish, he produced a beautiful magician's assistant, who was wearing gold lamé tights and was called Bébé.

BÉBÉ: Hullo Tommy, I'm a clue.

TOMMY: Are you? I suppose the rabbit is as well?

BÉBÉ: Of course, we're both in lots of places.

Then she disappeared with a puff of magic.

# THE HAT BOX

Tommy went north two intersections to have a look in the hat box, but when he opened it out burst Bébé again.

   BÉBÉ: There you are, I'm in the hat box as well, and I occur in the next place you should go.

   Bébé or bee beee occurs a number of times in a beehive,
33 and also the letter B *is in the place* you are looking for.

# BEEHIVE

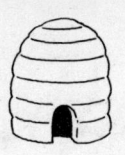

The beekeeper who tended the beehive on C6 naturally had not found the thingamybob that Tommy was looking for, but she did have some clues.

    BEEKEEPER: Nothing in my beehive except a lot of bees and some honey, do you get the point?

34  TOMMY: Ah, I see, there are *a number of points* on the thing I have lost.

35  BEEKEEPER: Quite right, and you could always *make a beeline for it from here*.

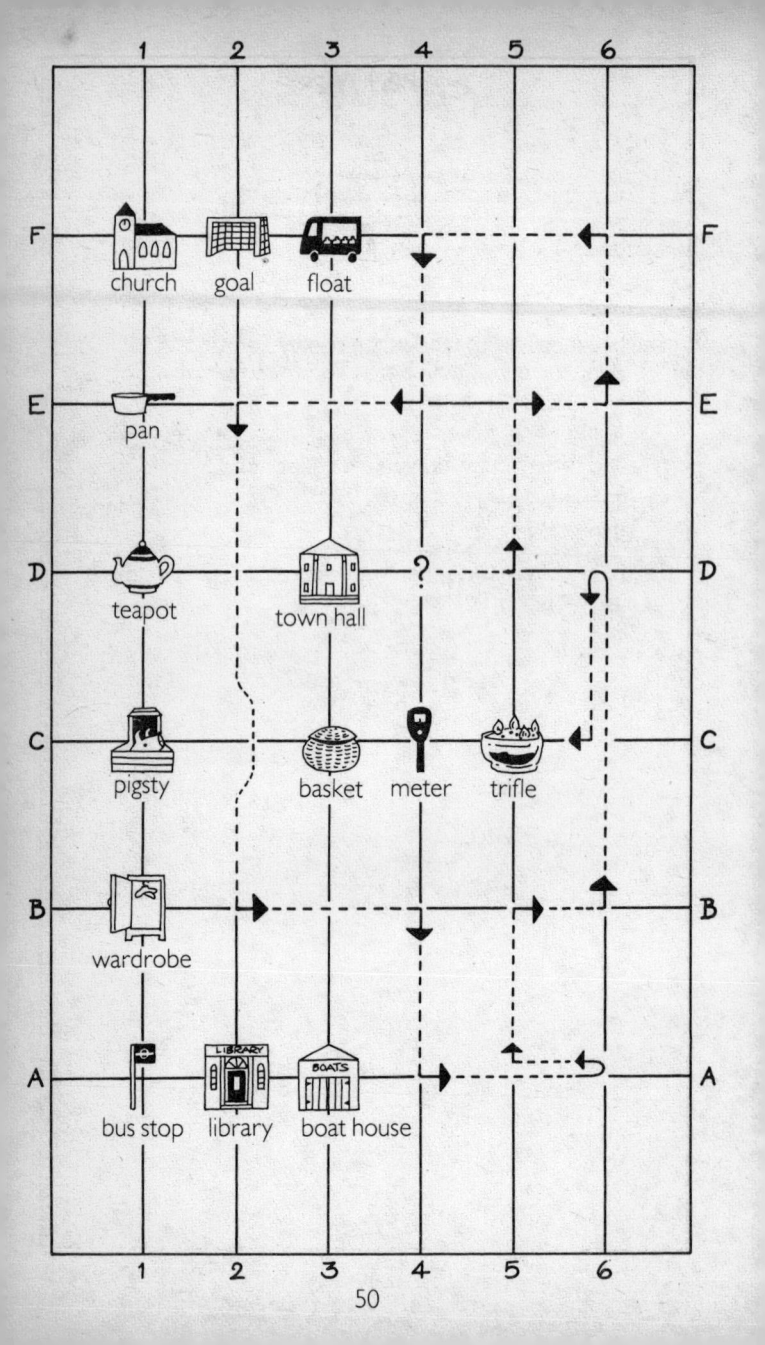

|   | 1 | 2 | 3 | 4 | 5 | 6 |
|---|---|---|---|---|---|---|
| F | church | goal | float | | | |
| E | pan | | | | | |
| D | teapot | | town hall | ? | | |
| C | pigsty | | basket | meter | trifle | |
| B | wardrobe | | | | | |
| A | bus stop | library | boat house | | | |

## NEARLY THERE!

You should have crossed off quite a few places on the grid by now:

The dotted line is the route you should have taken. The only place you can go next is the trifle. Possibly Tommy dropped his oojamaflip in that!

Over the page you will find all the clues so far to where the lost object could be and what it is.

## WHERE IT IS

*Somewhere with a T in it (9).*
*It is neither near nor far from the bridge (14).*
*There is a rabbit in it (24).*
*There is a B in it (33).*
*You can make a beeline to it from the beehive (35).*
*And the little old lady's poem clues (13, 23, 32).*

## WHAT IT IS

*It is bigger than a button (3).*
*It is bright and shiny (11).*
*It floated off in the opposite direction to that in which it was pointing (12).*
*It can go through the slot of a letter box (15).*
*It is round (19).*
*It has something to do with Bathurst (20).*
*The guide had one too (22).*
*Smaller than a dustbin lid (28).*
*It is very attractive (29).*
*It has something to do with NEWS (31).*
*It has a number of points on it (34).*
*And the odd ones out clues (2, 4, 5, 8, 10, 15, 26).*

You should have enough clues now to know what Tommy lost and where it is.

Tommy had got a little fed up with wandering round and round. By the way, that is another clue to what it is.

36  *It goes round and round*

37  The trifle on C5 only revealed a lot of things beginning with C like cake and custard, cream and cherries. *The lost thing begins with C but was not in the trifle.*

38  From C5 to C4 Tommy went to the parking meter, but the only help the parking meter gave him was to remind him of his lost object. *Something to do with a needle.*

************************************************************

## DID YOU KNOW...

that the first parking meter was invented by Carlton Magee for the city of Oklahoma in the USA in 1935. They were not introduced into Britain until 1958.

************************************************************

Talking about needles, like the ones which show how much time you have taken at a parking meter; Tommy then went to another place where there were needles.
39  Some were 1's and 2's and 3's and 4's like *knitting and sewing needle sizes* in the sewing basket owned by his dear old granny.

TOMMY: Have you seen my lost what's-it, Granny?

GRANNY: No dear, I haven't seen anything for a long time because I've lost my spectacles.

TOMMY: Oh dear, I wonder where they are?

40  GRANNY: Pass me my *bunny pin cushion*, dear. It is in the sewing basket.

He did so, said goodbye, and trudged off to the town hall to see if the mayor could help.

MAYOR: I know everything that goes on in this town, Tommy. A mayor has to know everything. That's why I
41  have a very *magnetic* personality, like your lost thing. If I were you I'd go back and see your granny again. You know where she is don't you?

Of course he did (so should you), and there he found his lost object, inside something with a T, a B and a rabbit in it.

What was the thing he had lost?

Well, if you don't know you look up the answers to the clues on page 108.

# GIRLS' BINGO

Can you fit each of the girl's names below on to the bingo card, so that you cover up all the meanings and get a full house?

| song | | flower | |
| --- | --- | --- | --- |
| fruit | coin | sunrise | |
| | name | | fruit |
| happiness | | month | colour |
| jewel | | | wood pin |
| musical instrument | | name | flower |
| jewel | | | rock |
| | name | US State | Australian town |
| | card game | flower | |
| colour | name | month | |

OLIVE   VIOLA   EMERALD   GEORGIA

GWEN   JOY

MAY   DAISY   RUBY   MARIGOLD   ROSE

LILY   DAWN   ADELAIDE   FAITH   CAROL

CORAL   PEG   PENNY   HOPE   PATIENCE

JUNE   CHERRY   VIOLET   GRACE

## **WHO COMMITTED THE MURDER?**

Somebody down at Conundrum Castle has committed a foul murder.

Lady Fussiebustle has been found smothered by a tea bag in the castle tea-room.

Inspector Fathomit has come along to investigate the case and question the six suspects.

'It is evident that the murderer did this horrible deed alone,' Inspector Fathomit said. 'I can tell you that when I interviewed the suspects and got their statements most of them told the truth.'

This is what each of the suspects said:

THE BUTLER: 'I did it.'
LORD FUSSIEBUSTLE: 'I was with the butler.'
THE GARDENER: 'The maid did it.'
THE MAID: 'The butler didn't do it.'
THE CHAUFFEUR: 'I was with Nanny.'
THE NANNY: 'I was with the Gardener.'

Do you know who killed Lady Fussiebustle? Inspector Fathomit did.

# CHEAT!

The class of nine pupils had a written test of four questions in geography. At the end of the test the teacher collected the papers and marked them. The teacher then called one of the pupils up and to everyone's surprise said: 'You were cheating throughout that exam. I saw you peeking and checking your answers with the answers of the other pupils that you could see. And your answers agreed with the majority that you saw on each question. What's more, your answer paper proves it.'

In fact, the pupil's answer paper alongside all the others' answers did prove who was cheating.

|  | QUESTION 1 | 2 |
| --- | --- | --- |
| ARCHIE | WRONG | RIGHT |
| BARBARA | RIGHT | RIGHT |
| CLIVE | WRONG | RIGHT |
| DAPHNE | RIGHT | RIGHT |
| ERIC | WRONG | WRONG |
| FREDA | RIGHT | RIGHT |
| GRAHAM | RIGHT | WRONG |
| HARRIET | RIGHT | WRONG |
| ISOBEL | RIGHT | RIGHT |

## SEATING ARRANGEMENT

It was possible during the test that a pupil could only see the answer papers of the pupil next to them, immediately in front or diagonally in front of them.

WHICH PUPIL WAS THE CHEAT?

| 3 | 4 | POINTS |
|---|---|--------|
| WRONG | WRONG | 1 |
| RIGHT | WRONG | 3 |
| WRONG | RIGHT | 2 |
| RIGHT | RIGHT | 4 |
| RIGHT | RIGHT | 2 |
| WRONG | RIGHT | 3 |
| WRONG | RIGHT | 2 |
| WRONG | RIGHT | 2 |
| RIGHT | WRONG | 3 |

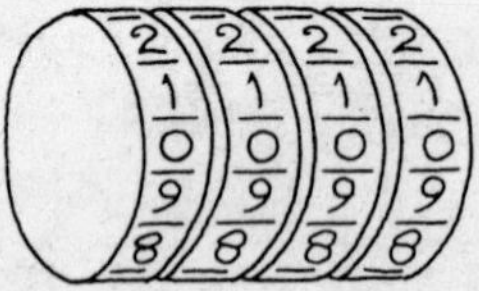
2
1
0
9
8
2
1
0
9
8
2
1
0
9
8
2
1
0
9
8

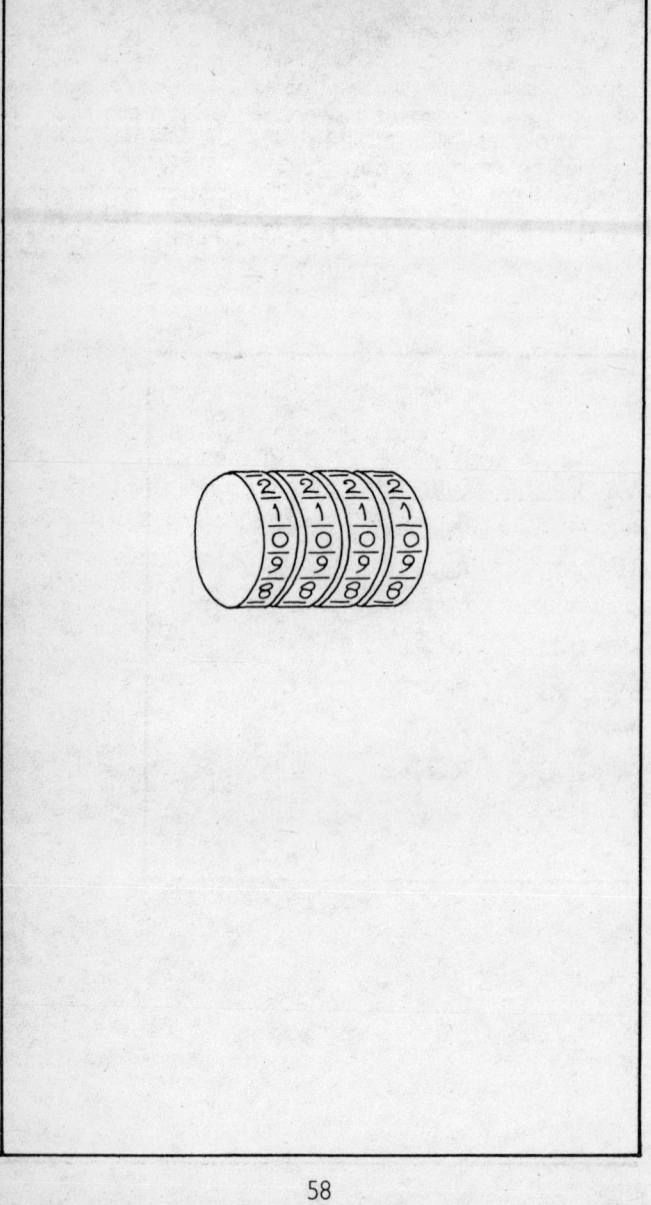

# THE PUZZLETON PLANS

\* \* \* \*

BECOME A BUDDING DETECTIVE AND FIND OUT WHAT HAPPENED TO THE SECRET PLANS AND WHO STOLE THEM

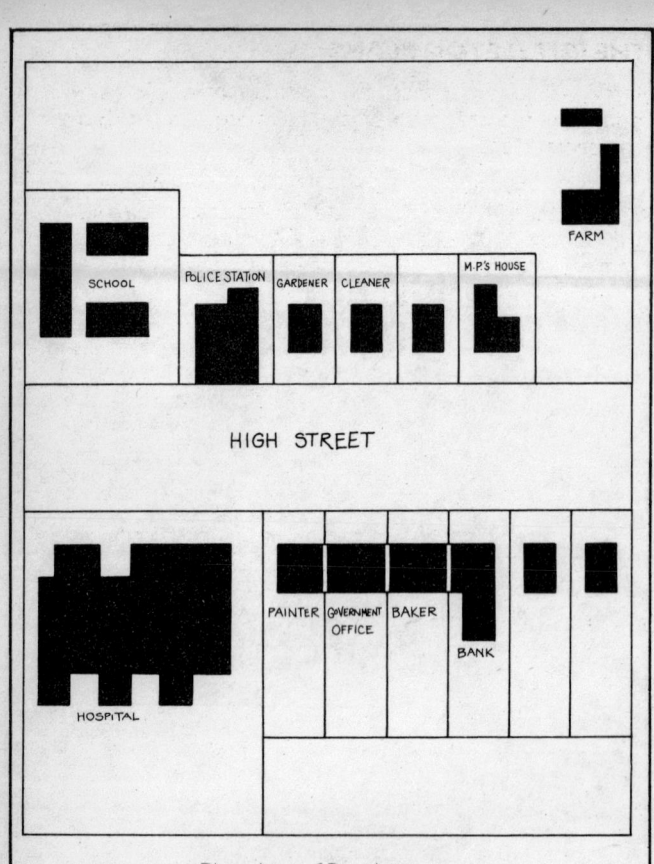

Plan view of Puzzleton town

# THE PUZZLETON PLANS

Kirsty and Howard went to the little town of Puzzleton in Riddleshire County to investigate the mystery of 'The Stolen Top-secret Plans'.

The Top-secret Plans were in the Government Office at 6 pm on a Tuesday evening and the MP reported them missing at 10 am on Wednesday morning. It is your job to find out from the clues on the following pages who stole them.

# THE SUSPECTS

| | | |
|---|---|---|
| POLICEMAN |  TRAFFIC WARDEN |  BAKER |
|  TEACHER |  PAINTER |  CLEANER |
|  BANKER |  NURSING SISTER |  FARMER |

MEMBER OF
PARLIAMENT

GARDENER

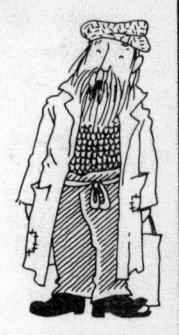

TRAMP

Kirsty and Howard had a lot of help from the inhabitants but found twelve of them a little suspicious. Strangely enough one of the suspects saw it all happen and later told everybody else, so although Howard and Kirsty did not know, and you do not know, all twelve of the suspects know who did it. Can you find out who it was? Remember, it all happened a long time ago.

Before you decide who looks the most suspicious, you had better decide for yourself what their names are. It's really quite easy to work out.

2 — MARK SPREADER
BOB COPPIT
IVOR MUCHMUNNY
DINO DAUBI
ROSA REE
NOELLE OTT
MRS GLAD TODOITALL
AVA TICKET
FLORA BUDD
POLLY TITIAN
JO HOBO
FRED BREDD

# 3      HOW THE PLANS WERE STOLEN

The Top-secret Plans were in a locked drawer in the MP's desk in the back room of the Government Offices at No. 10 in Puzzleton High Street. In the same drawer were some Non-secret Plans.

The thief came in through the window, which was open, and *using a torch* to see with, found the desk. This person, who was *wearing black gloves* so as not to leave fingerprints, then *forced the desk drawer open*, and took out both sets of plans. *Reading* that one was Top-secret and the other was Non-secret, the criminal put the letter back into the drawer and on top of it put *nine brand new coins* and *a little bit of mud*.

By the way, the thief was *wearing brand new striped socks*.

That theft happened a long time ago as you can see, and although the thief was caught everyone agreed to hush it all up. But the thief hid the plans. You have to find them as well!

# WHERE WERE THE PLANS HIDDEN?

In fact the thief did not exactly hide them, but put them away in a safe deposit box at the bank. You might ask, why doesn't the banker tell us where they are? Unfortunately Mr Muchmunny says he doesn't know, but they must be in one of the boxes numbered from 1 to 9999.

Mr Muchmunny also says that if you find the number of the box you will also find the number on the combination lock, because they are the same numbers. He has been even more helpful and said that if you started with a combination lock at 0000, the number you are looking for would *not be more than 9 clicks* of the lock wheels in either direction.

Here is a combination lock:

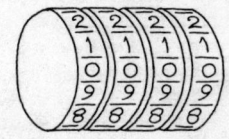

If you turned each wheel forward two clicks you would get the number 2222; if you turned them back two you would get 8888. Two forward and two back could give you 2288 or 2882 or 8822 etc. 9 clicks with the lock wheels could give you numbers like 6298 or 1075

## NUMBERS

Mr Ivor Muchmunny, the banker, also has said that nobody is allowed to choose the last 1807 boxes as he keeps those boxes for his own use. Howard quickly worked out that this meant the plans could be in a box between numbers 1 and 8192.

Now the interesting thing about the number 8192 is that it can be divided by 2. It can then be divided by 2 again, and then by 2 again and again and again until you are left with 1. In fact 2 × 2 × 2 × 2 × 2 × 2 × 2 × 2 × 2 × 2 × 2 × 2 × 2 = 8192. The number 8192 is going to be divided in half until we arrive at the right number.

# PC COPPIT'S STORY

Let us start by taking some evidence.

Kirsty and Howard first met the policeman, PC Bob Coppit, to ask him about the mystery.

> PC COPPIT: Well, of course I didn't do it, you must understand that. But, it could have been any one of the others. I mean, they were all in the Government Offices at some time or other between 6 pm on Tuesday and 10 am on Wednesday.
>
> HOWARD: How do you know?
>
> PC COPPIT: Well, I was there as well, wasn't I? You see I had to investigate all sorts of goings on. First there was the accident to poor Mrs Polly Titian. The painter had come round to sell her his new painting 'Black Rose-a-at Night'. She was having tea with the teacher, the banker and the farmer discussing plans.
>
> KIRSTY: What plans?
>
> PC COPPIT: After Dino Daubi had sold her his painting and put it up on the wall of the Government Office, he left. Only half an hour later it fell off the wall and knocked out the Member of Parliament for Puzzleton. I was called in with Sister Rosa Ree to take her to hospital, where she was kept until well past midnight suffering from shock. Just after midnight I was called back to the garden of No. 10 where I found Flora Budd and Fred Bredd having a terrible row.
>
> HOWARD: I know the baker's is next to the Government Office, but what was the gardener doing at No. 10?

PC COPPIT: You see, Flora keeps all the gardens tidy and nice in Puzzleton. And in every garden she has been experimenting with a highly secret project, that we all know about, her 'Black Rose'. One of her pure black roses had bloomed in the garden of No. 10 and she was there to tend to it. But it had been stolen. Cut off in its prime. Well, Flora immediately blamed Fred. He's very interested in roses. I sorted them out and, by the light of my torch, I did notice that the window of the office was open. Well I never! In the morning Mrs Glad Todoitall called me over to the Government Office, she was doing it all in the office, she always starts there. She pointed out old Jo Hobo asleep on the floor, he'd obviously come in to keep warm and had been in there all night. I saw him off the premises and passed Ava Ticket going in to collect her parking tickets. That must have been about 8 am. Later on that morning, of course, Mrs Titian discovered that the Top-secret Plans had been stolen. I knew, and so do you, that everyone had been there.

That was all that PC Coppit wanted to say. Although he knew who had taken the plans, he wouldn't say. It could have been him.

Kirsty and Howard decided to go and see the banker, Mr Muchmunny, and ask him more about the plans.

MR MUCHMUNNY: Oh yes, I was discussing Top-secret Plans with the MP, they were all to do with the bank. Anyway, I expect you want some help to find the right number of the safe deposit box and combination? I'll give you a clue.

*********************************************************

5             **BANKER'S NUMBER CLUE**

Remember, the number lies between 1 and 8192. Divide the number in half and choose one half by answering this question:

*Bobbies and coppers are slang expressions for policemen named after the founder of the police force, Sir Robert Coppah. Is that true or false? If it is false, choose the numbers 1–4096, if it is true, choose the numbers 4097–8192.*

*********************************************************

# THE TEACHER'S STORY

The second suspect that Howard and Kirsty talked to was Miss Noelle Ott, the teacher. Read carefully what she had to say:

NOELLE OTT: As Bob Coppit said, we all know who stole the plans, and I am going to give you a clue to who it wasn't. You can eliminate one of these two – the baker or the traffic warden – because one of them, the innocent one, always spoke the truth. I was driving to school on the Wednesday morning when I nearly ran over Fred Bredd crossing the street from his van to the baker's. Later I heard him arguing with Ava Ticket about the parking ticket she had given him. *He* said that he had driven off before 8.30 and *she* said she had come out of the Government Office at 8.30 and seen him parked at a meter without paying, so she'd given him a ticket. He said he was already at the school delivering bread by the time the school clock struck and she said she heard the clock as she left the office.

KIRSTY: That's not much of a clue, can I ask you some questions?

NOELLE OTT: Yes, and from my answers you can tell who was speaking the truth:

KIRSTY: What time do parking meters come into operation?

NOELLE OTT: 8.30 every morning except Sundays.

KIRSTY: Are there parking meters on the baker's side of the road?

NOELLE OTT: No.

KIRSTY: Does the school clock strike the half hour?

NOELLE OTT: Yes, it can be heard for miles.

KIRSTY: What time do you get to school?

NOELLE OTT: I always get in to school at 8.45 every morning.

The teacher's story certainly should have told you who was speaking the truth. You can eliminate that person from the list of suspects. There are now only eleven left.

While the teacher was helping she decided to give a clue to the correct box number. Miss Noelle Ott knows a lot, you know.

*************************************************************

### 7            TEACHER'S NUMBER CLUE

Now you know the number lies between 1 and 4096. Divide the number in half and choose one half by answering this question:

*If you have 3 red marbles, 3 blue marbles and 3 yellow marbles in a bag, how many do you have to take out, without looking, to make sure you have two of the same colour? If you think it is 4, choose the numbers 1–2048, if you think it is 3, choose the numbers from 2049–4096.*

*************************************************************

# THE BAKER'S STORY

*8*

The next person to tell a story was Fred Bredd, the baker. He was delivering biscuits to the Government Office at 6.30 on the evening of the Tuesday in question for Mrs Polly Titian's tea party, when the painter came round. He overheard everything they said, and this is his story:

FRED BREDD: Dino Daubi had brought round his painting of Black Rose-a-at Night to sell to Mrs Polly Titian. She liked his paintings, for some unknown reason. I mean, look at some of his work, I think it's very plain.

'Black Rose-a-at Night'

'White cat in snow'

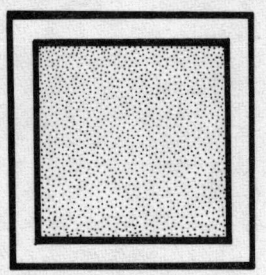

'Greyhound on a grey day'

FRED BREDD: Anyway, the MP liked Black Rose and thought it would be most appropriate to hang in the Government Office, as there was now a black rose growing in the garden. When Mrs Titian asked Dino how much the painting was, he said he wanted £900. She said that was very reasonable but wrote out a cheque for just nine *pence* only. I saw her do it! Well, poor old Dino can't read, he may be able to paint but he can't read.

He accepted the cheque without a murmur, hung the painting for her, and went. He didn't hang it up very well, because after we had all left it fell off the wall and knocked the MP out. I suppose that was justice really for her cheating Dino.

That was the end of Fred Bredd's story, and it did tell you that one of the two, the MP or the painter, had to be innocent of the theft of the plans.

Then Howard noticed that all the baker's biscuits had a rose motif on them.

FRED BREDD: Bit of a lover of roses myself. Biscuits are 9 pence each, do you want one?

There seem to be a number of things to do with 9 pence around Puzzleton. And the baker gave another clue to the box number.

\*\*\*\*\*\*\*\*\*\*\*\*\*\*\*\*\*\*\*\*\*\*\*\*\*\*\*\*\*\*\*\*\*\*\*\*\*\*\*\*\*\*\*\*\*\*\*\*\*\*\*\*\*\*\*\*\*\*

9             **BAKER'S NUMBER CLUE**

The number lies between 1 and 2048. Divide all those into two halves, and choose one half by answering this question:

*A lot of the people around here have double letters in their names, certainly the criminal has. But there is something strange about what each person likes to eat. For instance, Flora Budd likes pudding, Polly Titian likes jelly, and Rosa Ree likes sweets. What do you think Bob Coppit likes, potatoes or apples? If you think it is potatoes, choose numbers 1–1024, if you think it is apples, choose numbers 1025–2048.*

\*\*\*\*\*\*\*\*\*\*\*\*\*\*\*\*\*\*\*\*\*\*\*\*\*\*\*\*\*\*\*\*\*\*\*\*\*\*\*\*\*\*\*\*\*\*\*\*\*\*\*\*\*\*\*\*\*\*

# 10     THE TRAFFIC WARDEN'S STORY

The next inhabitant of Puzzleton to come up with a story was Ava Ticket, the traffic warden, whom you should have already eliminated from your enquiry. She was proved innocent by the teacher's story. So you should believe everything she has to say.

AVA TICKET: It was like this, you see, at the time of the theft I didn't know who had done it; I do now of course, but I always thought the two most suspicious characters were the cleaner and the tramp. After all, he had spent the night in the Government Office, sleeping on the floor and it was Mrs Todoitall who had found him there in the morning. I mean, old Jo could have taken them any time or Mrs T. could have stolen the plans before he woke up.

Anyway, by the time I had come back after my morning's work that Wednesday, to return all my ticket slips including the one I had given Fred Bredd, the MP had discovered the plans were missing, the policeman had gone and arrested Jo Hobo for illegal entry and taken him down the clink, and Mrs Todoitall had gone up to Mark Spreader's to do for him. I needn't have worried though, because the very next day when old Jo had been released I overheard him and Mrs Todoitall talking.

There was I, giving a few cars tickets outside her house, and she and Jo were talking about the previous morning. I was all ears. I heard Mrs Todoitall ask the tramp whether he wanted some new knitted striped socks. She knits everybody in the town striped socks and meant Jo to be no exception. She said she had noticed he had holes in the toes of his socks when she'd found him asleep in the Government Office. Well, all Jo said, apart from 'no thanks', was that he had holes in his boots as well, it sort of helped his feet to breathe or something. Mrs Todoitall insisted he went in for a cuppa and I'm sure she probably did knit him some new socks as well. I think she had plans for him. That's all there was to it.

So from that little story you should be able to eliminate yet another of the suspects, either the housewife or the tramp. Of course, the traffic warden had a clue to the number of the box as well. Here is her clue:

************************************************************

## 11    TRAFFIC WARDEN'S NUMBER CLUE

The number you are looking for is somewhere between 1025 and 2048. Divide those numbers into two equal halves and choose one half by answering this question:

*The first parking meter was introduced in 1935 in either Mayfair in London or Oklahoma, USA. If you think it was London, the number you are looking for lies between 1025 and 1536. If you think it was Oklahoma, choose the numbers 1537 to 2048.*

************************************************************

Are you any nearer solving the mystery of the stolen plans?

There are only nine suspects left now and it must be one of them who went into the Government Office wearing black gloves and new striped socks, forced open the desk drawer and took the Top-secret Plans. The number nine seems to have a lot to do with it. Also the criminal has a double letter in his name. Howard and Kirsty next tried to find out why some of the suspects were there at all that night.

The teacher, the banker, the gardener, the farmer had all said they were interested in plans. Even the nursing sister, Rosa Ree, was heard to say something about 'plans' when she'd gone to attend to the MP.

When they were asked to explain, this is what each one said:

NOELLE OTT: I went to discuss plans for Mrs Titian's children at school. You see, her daughter Martha May wants to be a dentist and her son Dennis wants to be an accountant. I said that because of their school results, it would be far better if Martha May Titian and Den Titian swapped subjects.

FLORA BUDD: You already know that I was much too interested in who had stolen my black rose to be bothered with plans. I tell you I think it was that baker chap who did it.

HOWARD: So the baker stole the plans?

FLORA BUDD: No. He pinched me roses. On the other hand it could have been that farmer who did it, I mean stole my roses. You see, I had asked him to bring some manure round to spread on the garden.

MARK SPREADER: That's right, I did bring some farm muck round to the Government Office garden, you know, Mark Spreader by name, muck spreader by nature. I tell you that when I was in the garden I had half a mind to go and see if I could find the plans in the office.

KIRSTY: What plans?

MARK SPREADER: Plans for a new paddock at my farm. The window was open. But I decided I'd pop along to the hospital and ask Mrs Titian for the key to the drawer.

ROSA REE: Yes, I did the plans want, having. Vhen Mrs Titian vas out-knocked by ze picture I vished ze plans to have, zey vould have helpen, so I took zem.

(Rosa Ree by the way is not English and always speaks like that.)

12  MR MUCHMUNNY: I went and had tea with the MP to discuss the Top-secret Government Plans for . . .

Well, he did not say what they were for, just said that everyone ought to find out for themselves. So now *you* have got to find out what the plans were for, where they have been hidden, and who stole them in the first place.

It was the tramp, old Jo Hobo, who suggested a game to play that would lead to the criminal straight away.

# ODD ONES OUT

Find the odd ones out in each line and with a little initial thought you will have a clue.

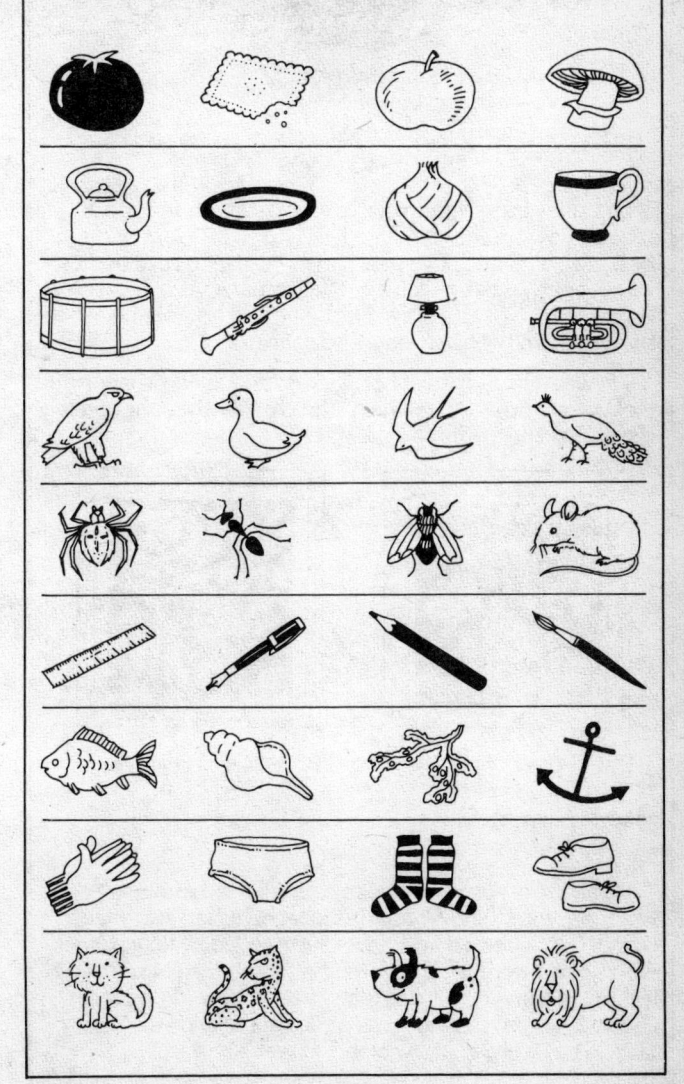

# THE PAINTER'S STORY

Dino Daubi, the painter, you have already met; and you should know that he could not have stolen the plans because he is unable to read. The thief had to be able to read because whoever it was had to tell the difference between Top-secret Plans and Non-secret Plans. Before he told his story he had to show off some of his wonderful paintings.

He was very sad about his 'Black Rose-a-at Night' falling off the wall and breaking, but he had two more plain black ones like these:

Black Rose at night
(study of the nursing
sister in her habit)

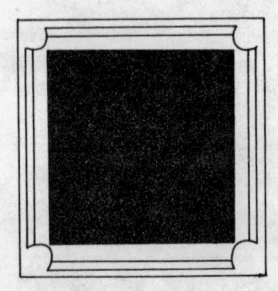

Black cat in a coal cellar

He also had a plain white one called 'Baker baking', which was supposed to show Fred Bredd from behind in a white overall with white hat and gloves surrounded by flour. Other works of art were: 'Red flag flying in sunset', 'Bluebird soaring high in the blue sky', 'Green tents in a meadow', 'Pineapple chunks in English custard', and 'Chocolate cake on mahogany table'. They were all plain colours as well.

DINO DAUBI: You have to-a use your-a imagination. My story will-a enable you to eliminate one of-a two suspects. The farmer or the cleaner. On the Wednesday after the robbery I was painting-a the ceiling of Senor Spreader's landing. Oh, it was the a-beautiful pink! It was pink cherubs eating strawberry blancmanges against a pink background, *magnificento!*

There was I, up-a on my planks, lying on-a my back painting, when Mrs Todoitall came round to do the cleaning. I-a heard everything she and Senor Spreader-a said. She asked him whether he had-a heard about-a the plans being stolen and he said he had not. He then-a told her all about-a my a-beautiful black-a painting falling down and knocking out Senora Titian. Gladys knew nothing of it, though she did-a say that my black-a painting was-a load of rubbish and it was a good job it had been broken. Quel cheek-a! They-a quite forgot I was-a listening. I will never wear her socks-a again!

KIRSTY: That was not much of a clue, Senor Daubi.

DINO DAUBI: I have-a not finished. The one who didn't-a know that the-a MP had been-a knocked out by my picture was innocent of the crime. Would you like to see-a two brand-a new paintings? I have-a gone into more-a detailed work.

'Zebra on Zebra crossing'   'Dalmatian dog playing on pebbly beach'

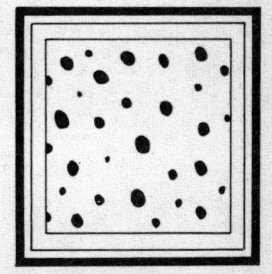

All you have to do is find out which of the two people Dino overheard did *not* know that Mrs Polly Titian had been knocked out, and then cross that person off the list of suspects.

HOWARD: When did all this happen?

DINO DAUBI: A long-a time ago, I remember painting a painting that year of the first landing.

HOWARD: Were they the pink cherubs on the landing in the farmhouse?

15 DINO DAUBI: No, no. The first-a landing on Mars, that-a was that-a year.

HOWARD: You're giving us so many clues you might as well give a clue to the number of the box.

*******************************************************

16 **PAINTER'S NUMBER CLUE**

The number you are looking for lies between 1537 and 2048.

*If I was-a lying I would tell you not to choose a number that is not-a lower than 1792.*

*******************************************************

## 17 THE BANKER'S STORY

The next story is from Mr Muchmunny, who had always been a prime suspect, as he knew all about the Secret Plans. When Kirsty visited the bank he was sitting there counting out money.

> MR MUCHMUNNY: 9999 pounds and 9 pence. That's the lot! By the way, the Secret Plans were called the Nine p. plans, because they were written in code.
>
> KIRSTY: What was the code?
>
> MR MUCHMUNNY: Oh, everybody knew that, because the MP had told us all. The Nine P stood for: 'Projected Precious Plans. Progressive Puzzleton Project Produces Perfect P...'
>
> KIRSTY: But what does the final P stand for?
>
> MR MUCHMUNNY: Nobody knew. The baker thought it stood for 'Pastry'. The PC thought it stood for 'Policemen'. The gardener thought it was 'Plants', the farmer 'Paddock', the teacher 'Pupils' and so on. I thought it was for 'Pounds' and I can tell you I was nearly right.

*Projected Precious Plans, Progressive Puzzleton Project Produces Perfect P...*

18   MR MUCHMUNNY: The day after the theft, my daughter Lotta overheard her teacher, Miss Ott, and the nursing sister, Rosa Ree, talking, and told me about it. Sister Rosa Ree said: 'I ze plans have stolen, Noelle, I had to do zis. Mrs Titian laid out and ze hospital she was needing. Zere zey were lying on ze floor, two of zem. Ze two plans were six feet long by six inches sick and ve carried your sick MP to ze hospital mit zem.'

Then Lotta said that Miss Ott also admitted taking some plan of action. I don't know what that could have been, but certainly I knew why my daughter had misheard what had been said, and I knew that one of those two ladies had not stolen the Secret Plans. Talking of nines again, I'll give you a clue.

*************************************************************

### 19              BANKER'S NUMBER CLUE

*If you divide the numbers from 1793–2048 into two equal halves you will find there are far more 9's in one set of numbers than the other. Choose that lot.*

*************************************************************

# THE GARDENER'S STORY

The gardener, Flora Budd, was a jolly old stick. She wore a big tweed jacket and a long tweed skirt, aptly rounded off by green welly boots. She was very helpful, but did like riddles, especially to do with gardening:

FLORA BUDD: Hello me old plum! Do you know how many peas there are in a pod?

HOWARD: It wouldn't be nine by any chance?

FLORA BUDD: No. There's only one 'p' in a pod, isn't there? Can't you spell?

I say, I know you are all wondering when this little mystery took place, aren't you? Well, I can tell you this: 'Chelsea Champions'. That was the year that my famous black roses won the Chelsea Flower Show supreme
20 Champion award. *Chelsea Champions.*

HOWARD: Well done, Flora, but can you give us more help?

21 FLORA BUDD: Simple, old bean. You know I was in the garden of the Government Office that night, don't you? Well, Dino Daubi had told me earlier that he'd sold his painting of my black rose to Polly Titian that very evening and it was hanging up inside. You see, old fruit, the window was open, so I just nipped in to take a look at it. It looked grand, all shiny, smooth and black, hanging there on the wall. He's a very sensitive painter is Dino. Then, crush my turnips, when I got back outside by the light of my torch I discovered my beautiful rose had gone, been stolen! The plant had been dug up deliberately. I knew who had done it of course, there were tell-tale signs. White all over the place! That Fred

81

Bredd can't go anywhere without leaving flour on everything. He always wears his white gloves and that's why he has to grow white roses. What's more there was PC Coppit poking his head over the fence. Old Coppit pops over and asks me what's the matter and I told him about my roses. He told me to run along and he'd investigate, so he switched on his torch and started to look about. I was highly suspicious that the PC was in on it too! I went round to Fred's leaving Bob Coppit nosing about at the back of the Government Office. Fred had the rose in a pot. He was copying its beauty to put on his biscuits.

She got her Black Rose back and went on to be Chelsea Champion. So that was her story and should have led you to eliminate yet another suspect. Before Flora went off to dig up some potatoes, she helped with the number of the box.

\*\*\*\*\*\*\*\*\*\*\*\*\*\*\*\*\*\*\*\*\*\*\*\*\*\*\*\*\*\*\*\*\*\*\*\*\*\*\*\*\*\*\*\*\*\*\*\*\*\*\*\*\*\*\*\*\*\*

22 **GARDENER'S NUMBER CLUE**

You should have narrowed the numbers down to one of the 128 numbers between 1921 and 2048. By dividing these numbers into two again you get 64 numbers between 1921 and 1984, and 64 numbers between 1985 and 2048. Which set are you going to choose with the next question?

*A type of plum called a greengage was named after a certain Sir W. Gage in 1725. If you think that is correct, choose the numbers 1921–1984, if you think it is not true, choose the numbers between 1985–2048.*

\*\*\*\*\*\*\*\*\*\*\*\*\*\*\*\*\*\*\*\*\*\*\*\*\*\*\*\*\*\*\*\*\*\*\*\*\*\*\*\*\*\*\*\*\*\*\*\*\*\*\*\*\*\*\*\*\*\*

Remember the number of the box you are looking for is the same as the number on its combination lock. If the combination lock was set at 9999 then the correct number would only be 6 clicks of the wheel away.

23 *Another interesting thing about the number is, that if you add all its digits up and then add the digits of that total together you will arrive at the number 9. For example the number 1 9 9 8 = 27 = 9 or 2 0 3 4 = 9*

# WHEN DID IT ALL HAPPEN?

All the people of Puzzleton remember the year when the Nine P plans were stolen – well, they cannot remember the *exact* date but they do know other things that happened that year.

If you remember the painter remembered it was the year that there was a *Landing on Mars*, and the gardener remembered *Chelsea Champions*, though that may have been something to do with football. The farmer, after he had built his paddock with the aid of the building plans, had a very special royal guest riding there that year, she was also voted *BBC Sports Personality* of the year. The policeman, who played tennis, remembered that the *Wimbledon Winner* was Evonne Goolagong that year. Dino Daubi, who sold his painting of 'Red flag at sunset' to the Russians said it was the year that *Kruschev died*, and the banker said it was the year that the *Persian Monarchy's Anniversary* was celebrated. All Ava Ticket could remember was that *Hot Love by T. Rex* was top of the hit parade and of course the MP remembered that it was the year that Britain did *Vote for Europe*.

You will find out the year is very significant. Especially when you consider what the Top-secret Plans were about.

# 25 THE NURSE'S STORY

Sister Rosa Ree was, as you should know, innocent of the crime:

> ROSA REE: It vas ze vay I am speaking. I ze vord got wrong. I did not ze plans take from ze Government Office, but ze planks, for to lie ze poor Mrs Titian on ze stretcheren. I vas in ze hospital mit ze MP, she vas very dazed. Vhile she vas zere, ze farmer Herr Spreader came to see her und I heard all zey said about planks, sorry I mean plans.
>
> Ze farmer, he vas vanting to see ze plans for his paddock again, ya? Vel, Mrs Titian told him ze vindow at ze back of ze Government Office vas of ze open. She told him he could slip in and look at ze plans, zey vere marked 'Not-secret Plans' and vere in a drawer in her desk mit some 'Top-secret Plans'. She gave him ze key to ze drawer and told him not to look at ze Top-secret Plans as nobody knew vhat vas in zem, not even her. Herr Spreader left my hospital at 11.30 pm and only ze half-hour later ze Polly Titian vas discharged.
>
> I sink zat from vhat I have just you been telling, you vill now know zat one of zose two persons didn't do zee stealing.

That is certainly true, especially if you look back at the description of the theft as it happened.

> ROSA REE: By ze vay, I know zat ze plans vere stolen at precisely one o'clock in ze morning. I know zat because ze teacher, Noelle Ott, told me. But I do not know how she knows zis.
>
> HOWARD: Probably because Noelle Ott knows a lot!

ROSA REE: I vill recite to you a nursery rhyme. It has something to do with finding the number of the safe deposit box.

> Hickory dickory dock,
> Ze mouse ran up ze clock,
> Ze clock struck one
> Ze mouse ran down,
> Hickory dickory dock.

***

## 26     NURSE'S NUMBER CLUE

You only have the numbers between 1921 and 1984 to choose from now. Divide them into two halves and choose one half by answering the question:

*What is the most frequent letter occurring in the rhyme above? If it is 'C' then choose the lower numbers, if it is 'O' then choose the higher numbers.*

***

# 27 THE MEMBER OF PARLIAMENT'S STORY

Polly Titian, who has been Member of Parliament for Puzzleton for many years, told Kirsty and Howard the Party Policies that she introduced a week after the Plans were stolen.

POLLY TITIAN: My Party's policies – Polly's policies – are quite clear and I expect you to vote for me because they make sense. My Party believes in fair play for all and the truth. If I am re-elected I will make sure that the following laws will be enforced:
1. Only people who speak the truth will be allowed to vote.
2. All children with blue eyes will receive free school dinners.
3. All fines will be paid for in liquorice allsorts.
4. Top-secret Plans will always be kept in the right-hand top drawer of my desk from Mondays to Fridays.
5. All people with an 'O' in their name will be liable to more tax, an 'O' Tax.
6. Only persons with 9 letters in their name are known thieves and will be treated as suspect.
7. The letter 'P' will replace the letter 'D' ten times in every twenty-four.

These policies make sense, I know it, you know it, they know it. Vote for me, Polly Titian, now!

Even despite those ridiculous policies Polly Titian was voted in by the people of Puzzleton. Her laws were enforced immediately. Of course you all realise that Law No. 6 meant that nobody could suspect two of the people left on your stolen plans list. Polly Titian wasn't finished, she had another clue. She said the day after the election she had overheard the following conversation between the teacher, Noelle Ott and the policeman, Bob Coppit.

*28*  TEACHER: Hello, Bobby, nice to see you on duty.

PC: Glad to see you Noelle, I've been on duty all day.

TEACHER: So have I, at school from 8.45 in the morning to 4.30 in the afternoon.

PC: Did you vote yesterday?

TEACHER: Of course, I'm a great supporter of Polly Titian and the Puzzle Party.

PC: So am I, I always vote for her.

TEACHER: Didn't you say you were related to her?

PC: Sort of – her father's sister married my widow's brother.

TEACHER: Quite extraordinary, because my father's sister married her brother's father-in-law.

PC: We must be sort of related then.

TEACHER: No, I don't think so.

PC: Terrible business about the secret plans being stolen last week, wasn't it?

TEACHER: I know, I know that the plans were stolen at one in the morning.

PC: Mm! I wasn't anywhere near the Government Office at one o'clock.

TEACHER: Nor was I, I didn't take the plans.

And that was the end of the politicians's story, except she did say that if you read their conversation carefully one of them was obviously telling lies and naturally wouldn't have voted for her. The other is obviously innocent of the crime and can be struck off the list.

## 29             MORE NUMBERS

You should have by now narrowed the number down to the 32 numbers between 1953 and 1984. If you halve the numbers again and put the lower ones on the left and the higher on the right you will have two sets of sixteen numbers. If you halve each of these sets and put the lower 8 on the left and the higher 8 on the right you will have four sets of 8 numbers. The number you want is in the third set from the left.

By the way the number you are looking for is, in fact, the same as the year in which this all happened.

Before the last story – the tramp's story – is told, here is a recap. of all the clues you need:

*The number 9 is very important.*
*There are 9 letters in the thief's name (27).*
*The digits of the year added up twice comes to 9 (23).*
*The plans had something to do with 9 P (17).*

30     The thief actually lives at No. 9 Puzzleton High Street. See if you can work out where that is.

If you write down all the clues to the year it happened you will find another clue to the criminal:

*Landing on Mars*
*Chelsea Champions*
*BBC Sports Personality – Princess Anne*
*Wimbledon winner – Evonne Goolagong*
*Kruschev died*
*Persian Monarchy 2500 years old*
*Hot Love by T. Rex No. 1*
*Vote for Europe (24)*

And all the odd ones out on page 75 gave a clue with their initials.

88

# THE TRAMP'S STORY

*31*

The only person who knew who had done the dirty deed from the start, apart from the criminal, was Jo Hobo the tramp.

> JO HOBO: It was a cold night, so about eleven o'clock I popped into the garden of the Government Office. I saw that the window was open, so I went inside where it was warm, curled up behind the sofa and fell asleep.
>
> I was woken up by someone climbing through the window. I heard the school clock strike one. I thought it might have been striking the half-hour, but the teacher told me later that if I heard another strike of one that would be half-past one, because the school clock strikes one bell on the half as well. The person who entered took off their boots and walked to the desk in their striped socks. They then broke open the drawer and took out the Top-secret Plans. Inside the plans were some new coins which they left behind. The thief was definitely a woman.

And that's an end to it. You should now know who stole the plans and what year, what box number and what combination number it was.

> The number was certainly one of these:
> *32* 1969 1970 1971 1972 1973 1974 1975 or 1976

The answers to the clues are on page 112.

## ODD ONES OUT

The first letter of each of the odd ones out in each line spell out an animal, what is it?

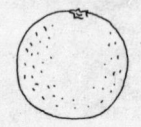

# DECODE IT

The plan shown below of a country mansion and stables is all in code. So are the instructions which will lead you to a hoard of treasure.

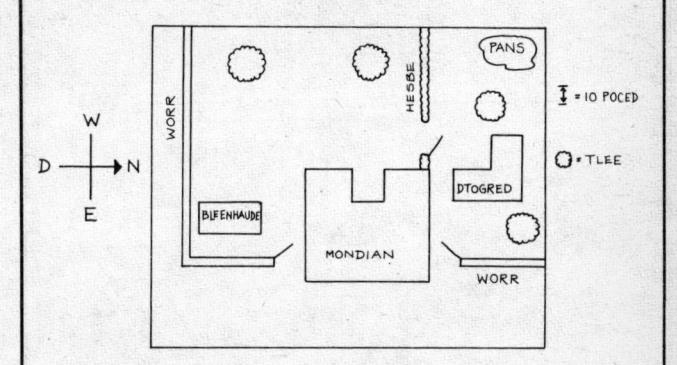

```
                                    PANS
         WORR           HE SBE
                                         I = 10 POCED
 W
D -+- N                                  O = TLEE
 E
                              DTOGRED
         BLFENHAUDE
                    MONDIAN
                                    WORR
```

    INDTLUCTIAND
BA THLAUGH THE BOTE. WORK TA THE TORR TLEE
AN YAUL REFT.
TULN DAUTH, WORK UNTIR YAU CON BA NA
FULTHEL.
TULN NALTH-EODT ONSYWORK TA O CALNEL.
WORK LAUNS TWA MALE CALNELD ONS YAU WIRR
GE FOCIND EODT.
TOKE TEN POCED ONS YAU HOVE FAUNS THE BARS
GOLD, DA SIB THEM UP.

Luckily I can tell you the two key words. They are GOLD and BARS, i.e. the letters of GOLD are replaced by the letters of BARS and vice versa, throughout the 'INDTLUCTIAND'.

Can you find where the gold bars are hidden?

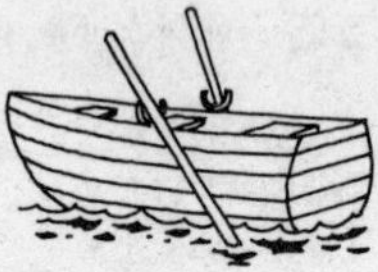

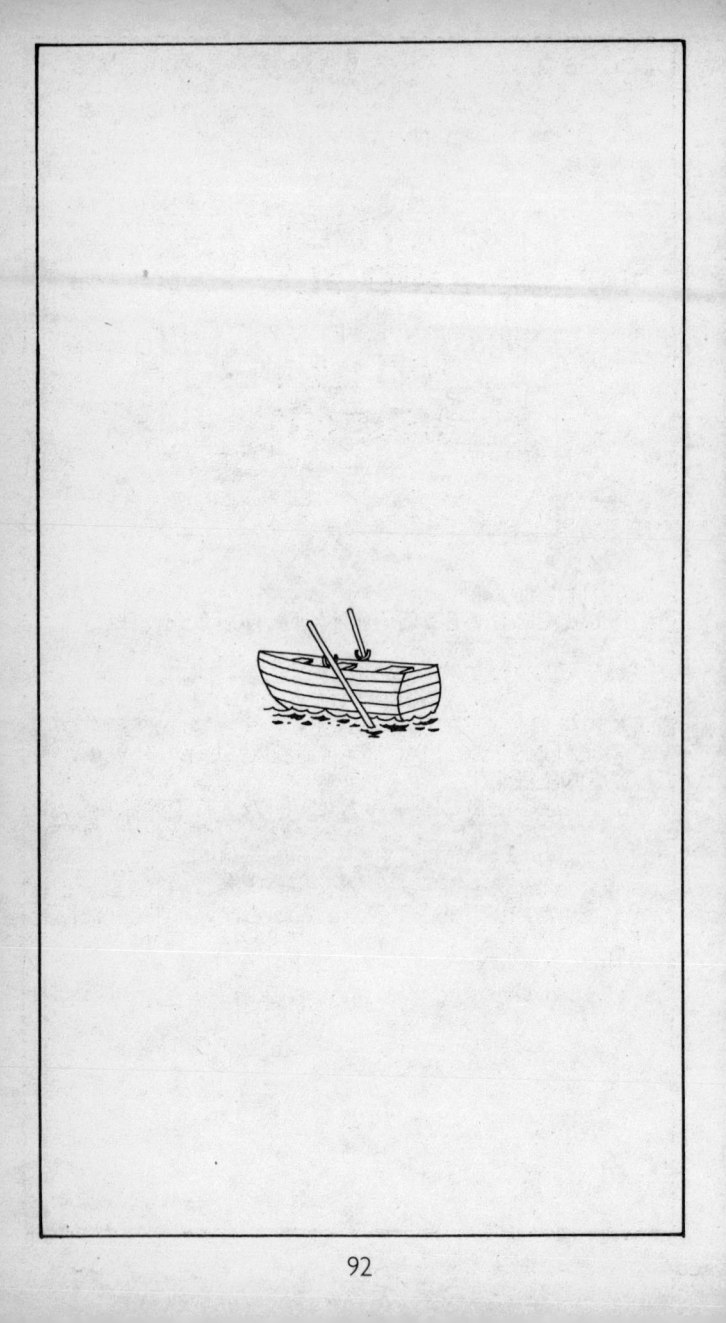

# THE RIDDLE OF SKULLY ISLAND

\* \* \* \*

SOLVE THE MYSTERY OF
THE ISLAND AND THE
HIDDEN TREASURE

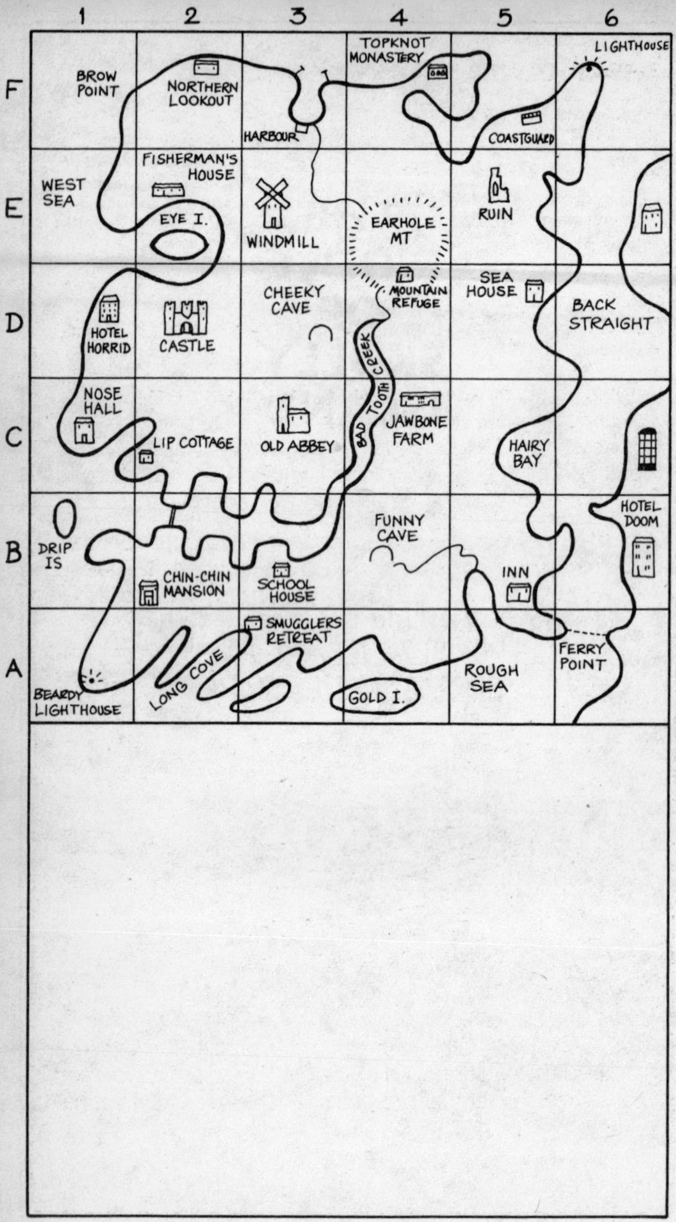

1
2
3
4
5
6
F
E
D
C
B
A
BROW POINT
NORTHERN LOOKOUT
HARBOUR
TOPKNOT MONASTERY
LIGHTHOUSE
COASTGUARD
WEST SEA
FISHERMAN'S HOUSE
EYE I.
WINDMILL
EARHOLE MT
RUIN
HOTEL HORRID
CASTLE
CHEEKY CAVE
MOUNTAIN REFUGE
SEA HOUSE
BACK STRAIGHT
NOSE HALL
LIP COTTAGE
OLD ABBEY
BAD TOOTH CREEK
JAWBONE FARM
HAIRY BAY
DRIP IS
CHIN-CHIN MANSION
SCHOOL HOUSE
FUNNY CAVE
INN
HOTEL DOOM
SMUGGLERS RETREAT
LONG COVE
BEARDY LIGHTHOUSE
GOLD I.
ROUGH SEA
FERRY POINT

# THE RIDDLE OF SKULLY ISLAND

When Davy Jones and Eileen Fletcher were on holiday staying at Hotel Doom, they found the old map shown opposite. It is of Skully Island and, as you can see, it is aptly named.

It is a treasure map of course, but all that Davy and Eileen know is that the treasure is hidden in one of the buildings on the map. Which building in which square? And when you get to the right spooky place in which room has the treasure been hidden? What is more, can you find out who has hidden the treasure?

On their adventures the two puzzle solvers meet a number of strange characters. They are:
Igor Roland, Mr Dungo, Father Righteous, Sir Crackpot, Noel Nose, Percy the Punk, Lady Chin-Chin, Betty Ballast, Mrs Seetoem, Miss Stern, Gladys Gull and Wanda Sweet.

Each of them will give you a clue to the building where the treasure is hidden. Then, when you have worked that out, they will each give another clue to what room it is hidden in.

1  IGOR: Hello there, I am the ferryman and I know all about the terrible Skully Island. My clue is simply this: *you can row to the square.*

2  LADY CHIN-CHIN: I'm very rich, you know, I live in Chin-Chin Mansion. Of course, as you are so clever, you will realise that the treasure is *not in a square that has no building in it.*

3 MR DUNGO: I run my farm on C4. The square you're looking for is *not in any square diagonally in line with my farm.*

4 BETTY BALLAST: I am a barmaid and I work at Sea House, I am well known for being very honest. I can tell you that the treasure is in *a square which is west of the castle.*

5 FATHER RIGHTEOUS: I am a priest. All I will tell you is that *Betty Ballast always tells lies.*

Davy and Eileen knew they had to believe a monk.

6 MRS SEETOEM: I own Sea House, a very nice boarding-house, and Betty certainly does not work there, she serves at the Inn on B5. I can tell you the treasure is *nearer to Sea House, than it is to Chin-Chin mansion.*

7 SIR CRACKPOT: I am a Knight and live at the castle on D2. Oh dearie me, what was my clue? Oh? No, it's O, that's it. There is an O in the place you want to go. Oh, dearie me!

MISS STERN: Naturally, you know who I am, I'm the school teacher and I teach at the school house on B3. Clever old stick, I am. I've worked this out and so must
8 you. *The square you want is not more than five squares from the school house.*

NOEL NOSE: Hello, I live in Nose Hall, named after me
9 you know. I can tell you that *one of the people who has already talked to you lives at the place.*

GLADYS GULL: I'm a bird watcher and I go all round the
10 island, *watching things. I live in Lip Cottage.*

11 PERCY THE PUNK: I am the coastguard. I dress like a punk because I like to annoy people. So I am going to annoy you with my clue. Listen to this: *if I walked in a straight line from my coastguard station along row F or down column 5, and then I turned left, along another row or column, and left again along another I would get to where the treasure is hidden.*

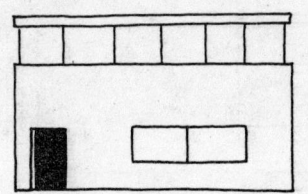

WANDA SWEET: You might think I am a sweet little old lady, but in fact in my spare time I'm a nasty old witch and I live in a mountain refuge. Here, do you want a sweet from Wanda Sweet?
12     *May I help you with this case?*
    *One of us lives at the Treasure Place,*
    *Nobody else is mentioned here;*
    *Keep the first and he will appear.*
By the way, it is a very solitary place next to where I live. Good luck!

97

Well, Davy and Eileen certainly knew which building the treasure was in, do you?

If you don't, then you had better look up the answers on page 118.

On page 119 is a plan view of the building, so don't cheat and look before you have guessed where it is. By the way, all the characters that you have already met were at the place and they all gave clues to which room the treasure is in and who hid it there.

This is the inside of the building. There are ten places the treasure, which was some valuable jewellery, could be hidden. In the *hall, lounge, dining-room, kitchen, conservatory, toilet, office, library, waiting-room* or *chapel*.

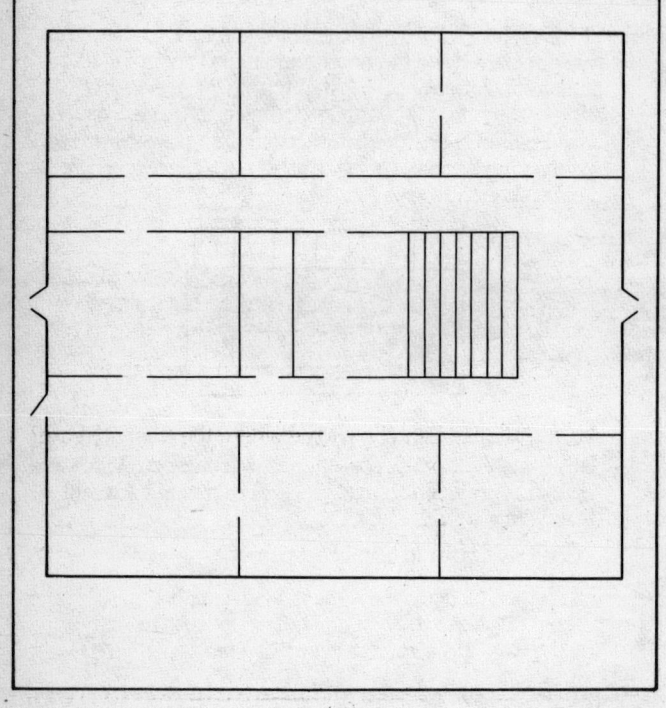

To help you know which room is which, here is some information:

13  The *toilet* is of course the smallest room.
    The *conservatory* is at the back.
    The *chapel* lies between the *library* and the *office*.
    The *dining-room* is opposite the *waiting-room*.
    When you enter through the front door into the *hall*, the *lounge* is immediately on your left.
    The *kitchen* is next to the *dining-room*.
    The *library* has only one door.

Davy and Eileen met all the characters again over dinner in the dining-room. As before they all told the truth except one.

14  IGOR ROLAND: The jewellery is not in the *hall*.

15  LADY CHIN-CHIN: *Father Righteous*, himself, doesn't know who hid it.

16  MR DUNGO: It wasn't me.

17  BETTY BALLAST: One of us ladies did it.

18  FATHER RIGHTEOUS: Nobody here, except me, has been in the *chapel*.

19  MRS SEETOEM: You *have* to go through two doors to get to where the jewellery is hidden.

20  SIR CRACKPOT: I say, oh dearie me, the room you're looking for has got an *O* in it, as well, so has the person you're looking for. Well I never, oh dearie me!

21  MISS STERN: It is not in a room which is next to the *toilet*.

22  NOEL NOSE: Can you tell me where the *toilet* is please?

23  GLADYS GULL: Certainly, go out that door, turn left down the corridor and it's the first door on your right. Did you know the person who hid the jewellery has the same initial letter in both their names?

24 PERCY THE PUNK: I've got another complicated and annoying clue, because I'm like that. If you go out *one of the doors from here*, then *go through another door*, there will be one opposite you. Go *through that and turn left*. Go through the *next door* which is *immediately in front of you* and turn *left* again. Turn *left again* and go *through the first door on your left*. The door on your *right* is the *room you want*.

25 WANDA SWEET: Oh dear, why does Percy have to be so complicated?

> I wonder if a poem will aid
> Your search? You've done enough
> With calculations you have made,
> You'd better now, call the whole thing off,
> I certainly would, if I were you,
> If you don't see within this rhyme
> The room is written straight and true;
> Just look around and take your time.

From those clues you should now know where the jewellery was and who had hidden it there. As always, if you cannot work it out, the answers to all the clues are on pages 118-120.

# PICTURE PAIRS

You should be able to find twenty-five objects in this jumbled-up drawing. Twenty-four of them go in pairs and one is an odd one out, which is it? There is a pair of pears right at the top to start you going.

101

# ROUND UP

NINE QUESTIONS BASED ON THE NINE EXTRA PUZZLES THROUGH THIS BOOK. IF YOU ANSWER THEM ALL CORRECTLY YOU SHOULD HAVE SPELT OUT SOME TREASURED THINGS.

1. What the letter 'G' stood for in the secret code.
2. The common letter in:

3. Initial of the pupil who could not have cheated at all.
4. Initial of the girl's name which fitted the top left-hand square of the bingo card.
5. Last letter of this lady's name:

6. The shape of a sock.
7. The most frequent letter that occurs on page 90.
8. What room was Lady Fussiebustle murdered in?
9. What letter comes before 'q' on page 20?

# ANSWERS

## PUZZLE ISLAND

*The treasure was a piggy bank and it was in the tree trunk in square D5.*

The following explanation of the numbered clues is divided into two parts, those which appertain to the whereabouts of the treasure, and those which describe the treasure, with appropriate notes:

*Finding the square*
Each clue is followed by a list of the squares it eliminates or leads to:

| CLUE | SQUARES ELIMINATED | THOSE LEFT |
|---|---|---|
| 1 On dry land | No land in: A7, A8, B1, D1, D8, E8 F8, G1, H1, H2, H6. | |
| 4 Sharks | Surround B7: A6, A7, A8, B6, B8, C6 C7, C8. | |
| 5 Lion roams | Surround Northern Cave on F2: E1, E2, E3, F1, F2, F3, G1, G2, G3. | |
| | SQUARES POSSIBLE | |
| 6 In a trunk | Telephone trunk call: | H5 |
| | Elephant trunk: D2, F4 | D2 |
| | In a treasure chest: D7, E6, G4 | D7, E6, G4 |
| | Tree trunk: C3, C4, C5, D3, D4, D5, E3, E4, F4 | C3, C4, C5, D3, D4, D5, E4, F4 |
| | In building or ship: A1, B3, C3, C5, C6, E3, E4, F1, F7, G4, G6. | A1, B3, F7 G6. |
| | SQUARES ELIMINATED | |
| 7 No water in square | F4 | |

| CLUE | SQUARES ELIMINATED | THOSE LEFT |
|---|---|---|
| 10 Within 13 squares of Look-Out Point | Look-Out Point = H3 (see Look-Out Rd.) A5, A6, A7, B5, B6, C5. | A1, B3, C3, C4, D2, D3, D4, D5, D7, E4, E6, F4, F7, G4, G6, H5. |
| 13 Volcano erupts | North-east 9 squares: F6, F7, F8, G6, G7, G8, H6, H7, H8. | A1, B3, C3, C4, D2, D3, D4, D5, D7, E4, E6, F4, G4, H5. |
| 14 Windmill fire | C3, D3, E3. | |
| 16 Equidistant Spyglass Hill (F3 or D4) and Little Harbour (B3 or F7) | SQUARES POSSIBLE (F3 and B3): D1, D2, D3, D4, D5, D6, D7, D8. (F3 and F7): A5, B5, C5, D5, E5, F5, G5, H5. (D5 and B3): A6, B5, C4, D3, E2, F1. (D5 and F7): C8, D7, E6, F5, G4, H3. | C4, D2, D4, D5, D7, E6, G4, H5. |
| 17 Ants | SQUARES ELIMINATED North of lone tree in (C4): D4. | |
| 18 Marsh | F5 | |
| 21 Loch Bess Monster | Lake at E6 and E5 | C4, D2, D5, D7, G4, H5. |
| 22 Two Knight's moves | | Of those left: C4, D5, D7, G4, H5. |
| 24 Lighthouse | Offshore is at (A1): A1, A2, A3, A4, A5, A6, A7, A8, B1, C1, D1, E1, F1, G1, H1. | |
| 25 No path or road | | Of those left: D5, D7, G4. |
| 26 Coastline facing South | Has no effect on those left. | |
| 27 Ships fighting: | G4 | D5, D7 |
| 28 Midway Bridge (D3) and Sails (C3) | East from there: | D5, D7 |
| 29 No coastline | D7 | D5 |

105

*Describing the treasure*

## CLUE

- 2  It is hard and shiny.
- 3  A pig has four legs.
- 8  It measured 22mm × 15mm × 15mm.
- 9  When it is broken you can get at all the money.
- 11  The flowers were bright colours on it.
- 12  It has a 'tail'.
- 15  A collector's item for collecting coins.
- 19  A pig squeaks and a money box rattles.
- 20  A real pig can be found in a farmyard, a piggy bank on the mantelpiece.
- 23  The little piggy is the little toe from the rhyme:
    This little piggy went to market,
    This little piggy stayed at home,
    This little piggy had roast beef,
    And this little piggy had none,
    While this little piggy went wee, wee, wee, wee
      all the way home.
  You will notice that there is a River Piggy in square D5. The tree trunk is on the 'bank' of the River Piggy.
- 30  Oinkment is obviously what pigs need to soothe them.
- 31  Pigs are greedy, and those who hoard money are misers.
- 32  It is very easy to put money into the slot of a piggy bank but difficult to get it out again without breaking it.

## WHAT ANIMAL DID I MEET?

The CAMEL:
It does have an L in it, and is the only one with 2/3 of APE in it, i.e. A and E.

## WHO ARE WEARING THE SCARVES?

FREDA and EMMA:
The only definite identification that can be given is for ladies 2, 4 and 5: Freda, Emma and Deirdre.

## LOST AND FOUND

The object that Tommy had lost was his *compass* in the *sewing basket* at C3.

The explanations to the numbered clues are as follows:

*CLUE*

1. The bus is missing from C2.
2. Odd One Out: The *calendar* is the only one that starts with C (compare clues 4, 5, 8, 10, 16 and 26).
3. The object is 'bigger than a button'.
4. Odd One Out: *Oranges* start with O (compare clues 2, 5, 8, 10, 16 and 26).
5. Odd One Out: *Mackintosh* starts with M (compare clues 2, 4, 8, 10, 16 and 26).
6. The lost object starts with the letter C.
7. The object is not: keys, handkerchief, pencil, rubber, coins.
8. Odd One Out: *Pavement* starts with P (compare clues 2, 4, 5, 10, 16 and 26).
9. The place has a T in it (sewing baskeT).
10. Odd One Out: *Anchor* starts with A (compare clues 2, 4, 5, 8, 16 and 26).
11. The object is 'bright and shiny'.
12. The river runs downstream south from the bridge, a compass needle points north, so it is pointing the opposite direction to that from which it would float.
13. The first letter of each line of the little old lady's poem spells out the word SEWING (compare with clues 23 and 33).
14. If the place you are looking for is 'Not near or far from the bridge' at F5, you can eliminate the nearest squares, i.e.: F4, F6, E4, E5 and E6 and the farthest square, namely A1.
15. The object can easily be dropped through the slot in a letter box.
16. Odd One Out: *Sausages* start with S (compare clues 2, 4, 5, 8, 10 and 26).
17. A reference to Canada, compare with clues 20 and 21.
18. The lost object is not: a *key*, *penknife*, *buckle* or *coin*.
19. The object is 'round'.

| | |
|---|---|
| 20 | Bathurst. The name Bathurst is found in Canada (clue 17) and is Bathurst Island, approximately 75°N. 100°W., the location of the magnetic pole (clue 21) to which all compasses point. |
| 21 | Compare with clue 17 and 20. |
| 22 | A good girl guide like Gertie would have had a compass. |
| 23 | The first letter of each line in the poem spells *Basket* (compare with clues 13 and 33). |
| 24 | There is a rabbit in the place. You will not discover this until clue 41. |
| 25 | The 'grandmama' clue refers to where she is – at the Sewing Basket. |
| 26 | Odd One Out: *Stubs* start with S (compare all the Odd One Out clues: 2, 4, 5, 8, 10, 16 and 26, the initial letters spell out COMPASS). |
| 27 | Third row back is the C row, third seat in is number 3 = C3. |
| 28 | The object is 'not as big as a dustbin lid'. |
| 29 | A compass is 'very attractive'. Attracted to the north. |
| 30 | 1's, 2's, 3's, 4's, 5's etc. could be needle sizes (compare with clue 40). |
| 31 | NEWS also stands for north, east, west, south, the major points on a compass. |
| 32 | The first letter of each line in the poem spells out CTHREE (compare with clues 13 and 23). |
| 33 | The place has a B in it (sewing Basket). |
| 34 | The points refer to the points on a compass (compare with clue 32). |
| 35 | A beeline is a straight line. C3 is in a straight line from the beehive at C6. |
| 36 | The object 'goes round and round'. A compass needle spins round. |
| 37 | The same clue as clue 6. |
| 38 | There is a needle in a compass. |
| 39 | Knitting needles (compare with clue 30) or sewing needles. |
| 40 | Granny asked for her 'bunny pin cushion' which was in the sewing basket (compare with clue 24). |
| 41 | A compass is magnetic. |

## GIRLS' BINGO

The Bingo card can be filled up in a number of ways, but only if you assign the girl's names to the following descriptions:

Song = CAROL
Coin = PENNY
Sunrise = DAWN
Happiness = JOY
Musical Instrument = VIOLA
Wood pin = PEG
Rock = CORAL
US State = GEORGIA
Australian town = ADELAIDE
Card game = PATIENCE
Months = MAY and JUNE
Jewels = EMERALD and RUBY
Fruit = CHERRY and OLIVE
Colours = ROSE and VIOLET
Flowers = DAISY, LILY and MARIGOLD
Names = FAITH, GRACE, HOPE and GWEN

## WHO COMMITTED THE MURDER?

The MAID did
If any of the others had done it, three or more of them would have been telling lies.

# CHEAT

FREDA was the cheat.

From the results of the test and the seating arrangement the following facts can be extracted: Archie could not see anyone else's paper so could not have cheated.

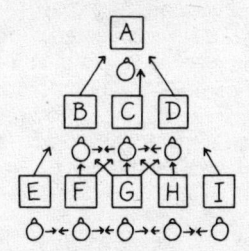

*Barbara* can see Archie and Clive, but in question 1 she answers 'right' where they both answer 'wrong', similarly with question 3.

*Clive* can see Archie, Barbara and Daphne, but in questions 1 and 3 he answers 'wrong' where both Barbara and Daphne answer 'right', and in Q4, Archie and Barbara answer 'wrong' and he answers 'right'.

*Daphne* can see Archie and Clive, but in Q1 and Q3 she answers 'right' while Archie and Clive answer 'wrong'.

*Eric* can see Barbara and Freda, but in Q1 and Q2 he answers 'wrong' while they answer 'right'.

*Graham* can see Barbara, Clive, Daphne, Freda and Harriet, but in question 2, four of them, Barbara, Clive, Daphne and Freda answer the opposite way to him, and in Q3, three of the five, Barbara, Daphne and Harriet answer 'right' and he answers 'wrong'.

*Harriet* can see Clive, Daphne, Graham and Isobel, but in Q2 Clive and Daphne and I answer 'right' and she answers 'wrong'.

*Isobel* can see Daphne and Harriet but in Q4 she answers 'wrong' while those two answer 'right'.

It is only *Freda* who never differs from the majority opinion of those she can see, namely Barbara, Clive, Eric and Graham.

# THE PUZZLETON PLANS

The person who stole the plans was the Gardener, Flora Budd. The number of the safe deposit box, combination lock and the year it all happened was the same, 1971. The plans were for the introduction of Decimal Coinage.

Your detective work according to each of the suspects' stories should have gradually eliminated eleven of the inhabitants of Puzzleton according to the numbered clues below. The box and combination number is similarly arrived at through the *Number Clues*. Clues to other events that happened in that year are liberally sprinkled through the Puzzle Trail. The nature of the plans is only reached by surmise.

NB: The black rose and the paintings are red herrings.

*CLUE*

1  First it was necessary to correctly identify the characters involved:

| | | | |
|---|---|---|---|
| Policeman: | Bob Coppit | Traffic Warden: | Ava Ticket |
| Baker: | Fred Bredd | Teacher: | Noell Ott |
| Painter: | Dino Daubi | Nursing Sister: | Rosa Ree |
| Banker: | Ivor Muchmunny | Gardener: | Flora Budd |
| Cleaner: | Gladys Todoitall | Tramp: | Jo Hobo |
| Farmer: | Mark Spreader | Member of Parliament: | Polly Titian |

2  The Government Office is Number 10. Other house numbers can be worked out with reference to clue 30.

3  From the description of the crime you must note the following: the torch indicates the crime took place at night; the thief was wearing *new* striped socks and black gloves. The thief read the two titles of the plans. Nine new coins were left by the thief. Drawer forced open and mud left inside.

4  The number 1971 is less than 9 clicks round on a combination lock from 0000.

5  *Number Clue:* It is false. Sir Robert Peel founded the police force. 'Copper' comes from the word 'cop', to catch (choose 1–4096).

6  If the teacher gets to school at 8.45 am, the baker was obviously parked at a meter opposite the Government Office at 8.30. He was lying. *Ava Ticket is eliminated.*

7  *Number Clue:* You must remove at least four marbles to make certain you have two marbles of the same colour (choose 1–2048).

8  If Dino could not read he could not have chosen the Top-secret Plans from the Not-secret Plans. *Dino Daubi proved innocent.*

9  *Number Clue:* Bob Co'PP'it must like a'PP'les. Each of the others likes something that has the same double letter in it as their name (choose 1025–2048).

10  Jo Hobo had holes in his stripy socks, the thief had new stripy socks. Compare clue 3. *Jo Hobo proved innocent.*

11  *Number Clue:* Parking meters were first introduced in Oklahoma, USA. They were not introduced in London until 1958 (choose 1537–2048).

12  By the way, the banker had to know the plans for the introduction of decimal coinage.

13  Odd Ones Out: Biscuit (the others grow). Onion (you can eat it). Lamp or Lantern (the others are musical instruments). Duck (the other birds can't swim). Fly (the only one that can). Ruler (you can draw or paint with the others). Anchor (man-made). Underpants (the other pairs consist of two things). Dog (not a member of the cat family).
The initial letters of the Odd One Out spell out BOLD FRAUD which is an anagram of FLORA BUDD, the criminal.

14  The cleaner, Mrs Glad Todoitall, did not know that Polly Titian had been knocked out by the painting. *Gladys Todoitall is eliminated.*

15  Clue to Year: The first landing on Mars was made by the Russian Mars 2 on 19 May. It actually crash landed, but Mars 3 soft-landed nine days later. (Compare all year clues at clue 24).

16  *Number Clue:* If Dino was telling the truth, he would say: 'Choose a number not lower than 1792', i.e. above 1792 (choose 1792–2048).

17  The 9 P. *Projected Precious Plans. Progressive Puzzleton Project Produces Perfect P.* The P stands on its own for P or Pence. The introduction of new decimal coinage pence: P instead of the old D.

18  Rosa Ree was talking about 'planks' not 'plans'. She was apt to mis-pronounce things. *Rosa Ree proved innocent.*

19  *Number Clue:* 50 nines occur in the numbers between 1793 and 1920. 101 nines occur in the numbers between 1921 and 2048 (choose 1921–2048).

20  Clue to Year: The Chelsea Flower Show is held every year but Chelsea Football Club won the European Cup-winners' Cup in 1971 (see clue 24).

21  All *budding* detectives should have noticed that Flora Budd incriminates herself here. She could not have popped in to the Government Office and seen Dino Daubi's painting 'Black Rose-a at Night', hanging on the wall, as it had already fallen down and knocked out the MP and was broken and Flora was carrying a torch. *Flora Budd incriminated.* In her own story she mentions that Fred Bredd always wears white floury gloves, the thief wore black gloves (see clue 3). *Fred Bredd proved innocent.*

22  *Number Clue:* This is true; Sir W. Gage did give his name to the greengage. (choose 1921–1984).

23  *Number Clue:* 1971 digit total = 18. 18 digit total = 9.

24  Year Clues: All the events below happened in 1971.
Landing on Mars – according to the painter (clue 15)
Chelsea Champions – according to the gardener (clue 20).
BBC Sports Personality – Princess Anne
Wimbledon Winner – Evonne Goolagong, according to the policeman.
Kruschev died – Leader of the USSR died on 11.9.71.
Persian Monarchy – 2500 years of the Persian monarchy celebrated.
Hot Love by T. Rex – Top of the hit parade six weeks, 20.3.71–24.4.71.
Vote for Europe – Britain voted to join the EEC, following referendum
1971 was also, of course, the year that decimal coinage was introduced.
The seventh letter in each of the headlined events above spells out: *gardener*.

25  The farmer did not need to force open the drawer (see clue 3), he had been given the key. *Mark Spreader proved innocent.*

26  *Number Clue:* The letter O occurs 12 times in the rhyme, the letter C only 11 times (choose 1953–1984).
27  Compare Polly Titian's Law 1 with clue 28. Although Law 5 is a clue – O is in the criminal's name – all suspects who are left have an O in their names.
Law 6: Persons with nine letters in their names are still suspect.
*Ivor Muchmunny and Polly Titian herself are eliminated.*
28  PC Bob Coppit was lying – his father's sister could not marry her own widow's brother, otherwise he would be dead! *Noelle Ott is eliminated.*
29  *Number Clue:* Dividing the numbers left into four groups as instructed: 1953–1960, 1961–1968, 1969–1976, 1977–1984. The third group from the left is 1969–1976 (choose 1969–1976).
30  Only Bob Coppit and Flora Budd are left as suspects. House Number 9 could only belong to Flora Budd, see Puzzleton Plan of house numbering (compare with clue 2)

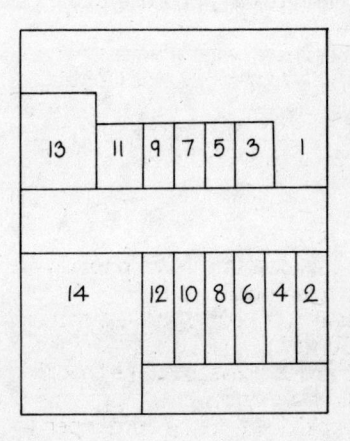

| 13 | 11 | 9 | 7 | 5 | 3 | 1 |

| 14 | 12 | 10 | 8 | 6 | 4 | 2 |

*31* The thief was definitely a woman: *Flora Budd finally incriminated,* FLORA BUDD WAS THE THIEF.

*32* Only 1971 obeys the rule for clue 23. 1971 is also the year it all happened.

Flora Budd, the gardener, thinking that the Projected Plans were to 'Produce Perfect Plants', stole them leaving the 9 coins, which were samples, behind. She was disturbed by the Policeman investigating the stolen roses. Jo Hobo saw it all. Flora came in through the window, took off her boots and tiptoed to the drawer in her new stripy socks. She had a torch to see with, and forced open the drawer with her trowel, hence the mud in the drawer. She was of course wearing black gloves.

## ODD ONES OUT

WOMBAT:
Wolf (the others are members of the cat family).
Onion (the others are fruit).
M (the other letters enclose space).
Bread (the others are dairy produce).
Ant (the others fly).
Table (the others have wheels).

# DECODE IT

X marks the spot where the hoard of treasure can be found:

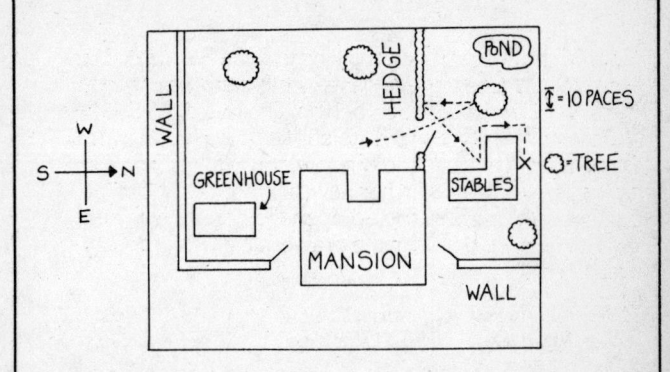

Substituting the letters GOLD for BARS and vice-versa, the code reads:

INSTRUCTIONS
GO THROUGH THE GATE. WALK TO THE TREE ON YOUR LEFT.
TURN SOUTH, WALK UNTIL YOU CAN GO NO FURTHER.
TURN NORTH-EAST AND WALK TO A CORNER.
WALK ROUND TWO MORE CORNERS AND YOU WILL BE FACING EAST.
TAKE TEN PACES AND YOU HAVE FOUND THE GOLD BARS, SO DIG THEM UP.

# THE RIDDLE OF SKULLY ISLAND

The building was the *Monastery* in square A4.

| CLUES | SQUARES ELIMINATED | SQUARES POSSIBLE |
|---|---|---|
| 1 Row to the square | No water in: D3 | |
| 2 No building | In: A2, A4, A5, A6, B1, B4, C5, C6, D4, D6, E1 and F1. | |
| 3 Diagonally from C4. | Not in: B3, B5, D5, E2, E6 and F1. | |
| 4 & 5 If Betty always lies, not in squares | W. of D2, i.e.: A1, C1, D1 and E1. | A3, B2, B6, C2, C3, C4, D2, E3, E4, E5, F2, F3, F4, F5, F6. |
| 6 Nearer D5 than B2 | Further: A3, B2, F2 | |
| 7 No O in: | Farm: C4<br>Windmill: E3<br>Ruin: E5<br>Castle: D2. | B6, C2, C3; E4, F3, F4, F5 and F6. |
| 8 Further than 5 squares from B3: | F5, F6 | |
| 9 The monk has already spoken | | |
| 10 Cannot be Lip Cottage: | C2 | B6, C3, E4, F3, F4. |
| 11 2 left turns from F5 cannot reach: | B6 | C3, E4, F3, F4. |
| 12 The first letters of Wanda's poem spell out MONK. A monk lives in a Monastery which is next to the Mountain on E4 . . . | | F4 |

118

## CLUES

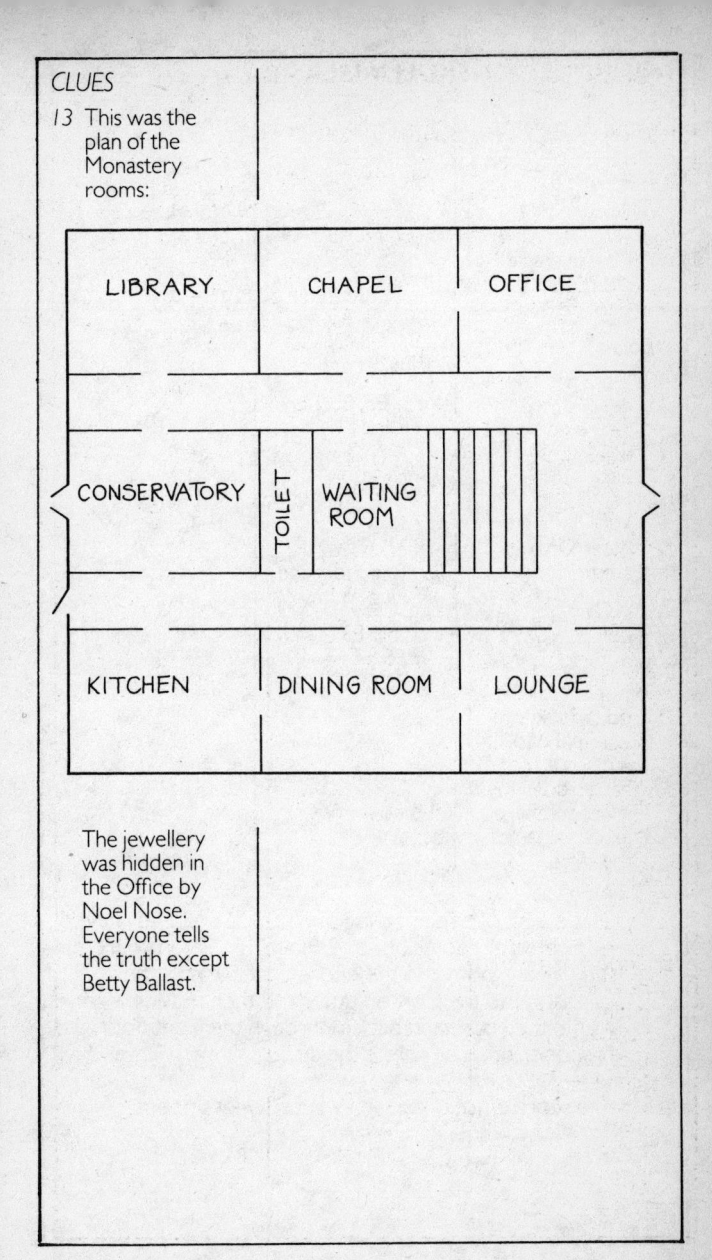

**13** This was the plan of the Monastery rooms:

| LIBRARY | CHAPEL | OFFICE |
|---|---|---|
| CONSERVATORY | TOILET / WAITING ROOM | |
| KITCHEN | DINING ROOM | LOUNGE |

The jewellery was hidden in the Office by Noel Nose. Everyone tells the truth except Betty Ballast.

| CLUES | ROOMS ELIMINATED | PERSONS SUSPECTED |
|---|---|---|
| 14 | Hall | |
| 15 | | Not Father Righteous |
| 16 | | Not Mr Dungo |
| 17 One of the ladies didn't do it. It must be: | | Igor Roland, Sir Crackpot, Noel Nose or Percy the Punk. |
| 18 | Chapel | |
| 19 Only one door is needed to get to: Three doors are needed to get back into: | Kitchen or Lounge Dining-room | |
| 20 No O in it: | Library | Not Percy the Punk |
| 21 Next to toilet are the: | Conservatory and Waiting-room | |
| 22 Noel Nose will be proved to be the correct suspect so if he does not know where the toilet is he could not have hidden the jewellery there. | Toilet | |
| 23 Initials of names the same: | | Noel Nose |

24  This is a bit of a red herring as you should already have eliminated all rooms but one. However, if you go from the Dining-room into the Kitchen, then across the corridor into the Conservatory and then outside, right round the house and back in through the front door, the first door on your right is the *office*.

25  The word *office* occurs in Wanda Sweet's poem:
"... the whole thing *off*
 I certainly would ..."

## PICTURE PAIRS

A SCREWDRIVER:
The other pairs are: 2 pears, a bat and ball, hammer and nail, club and spade, shuttlecock and battledore (badminton), cup and saucer, toothbrush and toothpaste tube, pair of socks, pepper and salt, brace and bit, plug and socket and an envelope and stamp.


## ROUND UP

BRACELETS:
1. B stood for G in *Decode it*.
2. R is the only letter that occurs in all of the following: parking meter, trifle, wheelbarrow, workman's hut.
3. Archie could not have cheated in *Cheat*.
4. Carol was a song in *Girls' Bingo*.
5. E was the last letter of Deirdre in *Scarves*.
6. L is the shape of a sock in *Picture pairs*.
7. E occurs 15 times on page 90 *Odd Ones Out*.
8. Tea-room was where Lady Fussiebustle was murdered in *Murder*.
9. S comes before q in Squirrel in *What animal did I meet?*

## ACKNOWLEDGEMENTS

The author wishes to thank all those who have helped in putting the five series of 'Puzzle Trail' on BBC TV. Especial thanks to Andy Johnson, Donna Reeve, Tommy Boyd, Sally Grace, Howard Stableford, Kirsty Miller, Davy Jones, Eileen Fletcher, Richard Simkin, Frances Gifford, Michael Forte, Ben Robinson and Malcolm Bird.

# More Clive Doig titles available from BBC/Knight

The Second Book of Jigsaw Puzzles

The Third Book of Jigsaw Puzzles

Jigsaw Puzzles 4

Three entertaining books filled with puzzles and word games, based on BBC television's award-winning *Jigsaw* programme.